DAISY'S
HOLIDAY COOKING

DAISY'S HOLIDAY COOKING

Delicious Latin Recipes for
Effortless Entertaining

Daisy Martinez

with Chris Styler

Photographs by Frances Janisch

ATRIA PAPERBACK

NEW YORK   LONDON   TORONTO   SYDNEY

ATRIA PAPERBACK

A Division of Simon & Schuster, Inc.
1230 Avenue of the Americas
New York, NY 10020

First Atria Paperback edition November 2010

ATRIA PAPERBACK and colophon are trademarks of Simon & Schuster, Inc.

For information about special discounts for bulk purchases,
please contact Simon & Schuster Special Sales at
1-866-506-1949 or business@simonandschuster.com.

The Simon & Schuster Speakers Bureau can bring authors
to your live event. For more information or to book an event,
contact the Simon & Schuster Speakers Bureau at
1-866-248-3049 or visit our website at www.simonspeakers.com.

Designed by Kyoko Watanabe

Food stylist: Alison Attenborough
Prop stylist: Deborah Williams

Manufactured in the United States of America

10   9   8   7   6   5   4   3   2   1

Library of Congress Cataloging-in-Publication Data

Martinez, Daisy.
Daisy's holiday cooking : delicious Latin recipes for effortless entertaining / Daisy Martinez with Chris Styler ;
photographs by Frances Janisch.
    p.   cm.
Includes index.
1. Cooking, Latin American. 2. Cooking, Puerto Rican. 3. Cooking, Spanish. 4. Menus. I. Styler, Christopher. II. Title.
TX716.A1M24   2010
641.598—dc22   2010026828

ISBN 978-1-4391-9923-7
ISBN 978-1-4391-9924-4 (ebook)

To my beautiful children,
Mookie, Skeets, Davyl, and Dodey

Thank you for allowing me to indulge my inner child.

CONTENTS

INTRODUCTION

For many people, the term "holiday entertaining" induces fear, if not downright terror. Everyone has heard a story or two of the beautifully browned turkey that is still frozen-raw on the inside, vegetables that are cooked until tasteless, or even, heaven forbid, lumpy gravy that tastes like schoolroom paste. Well, in the words of a familiar cartoon character, "Here I come to save the day!"

The recipes in this book are arranged by menus, each with a theme. This is not to say that a recipe (or even a menu) that is given for an autumnal holiday celebration wouldn't feel right at home on a winter holiday or an end-of-year party table. For example, the Mushroom-Plantain-Stuffed Chicken Breasts with Mango-Bacon Gravy found in the Cozy Festive Fall Dinner would be perfectly appropriate for New Year's Eve, and any one of the soups from the Open House Decorating Party could serve as a delicious first course in any other menu. You get the picture, right?

I've been able, through the years, to diminish my holiday-entertaining stress by applying a couple of important lessons I learned as a student at the French Culinary Institute in Manhattan: Whether you're cooking for six or for six hundred, the secret to a successful party is organization, organization, *organization*! With a bit of foresight and a few freezer-safe plastic containers and bags, you can minimize your last-minute kitchen duties, so that you can actively participate in the creation of your friends' and family's memories.

First, double up on recipes that freeze well (I let you know which these are right in the recipes) and get a leg up on future meals. Are you making soup for one of the menus? Do yourself a favor and make twice as much as you need, then freeze half and have the beginnings of an impromptu winter dinner with friends or a family meal on a night you're too pooped to cook. Making Mushroom *Picadillo* (page 13)? Make a double batch and freeze half. Keep the *picadillo* on hand for Mushroom Croquettes (page 59), a next-to-no-effort nibble to offer with drinks for friends who drop in to wish you happy holidays. The second lesson I learned is to prep foods as far ahead as I can without sacrificing quality. (Some foods—like soups and stews—benefit from

being made in advance.) Wash your salad greens and other components, and store in damp paper towels and plastic bags in the refrigerator. When it comes time for salad, simply dump, dress, toss, and serve! Throughout this book, in recipes and the preparation schedules that accompany each chapter, I point out what can be made ahead of time and how far ahead of party time it can be crossed off your list. *Heads up:* You'll notice that some of the make-ahead times in the preparation schedules don't match the make-ahead times in the recipes exactly. I grouped tasks together in the schedules in a way that makes the most sense to me. Feel free to fiddle with the schedules, as long as you don't exceed the make-ahead times given in the recipes.

I also like to differentiate holiday entertaining from events during the rest of the year by providing some memento for my guests, whether it's homemade, like the Mini-Morsel Mexican Wedding Cookies (page 70), or store bought, like a prettily wrapped bottle of good olive oil or vinegar. One year, at my Christmas tree–trimming party, I gave each of my guests an ornament for his or her own Christmas tree or Hanukkah bush; another year, I made *coquito* (page 151) and gave everyone a pretty corked bottle to take home. Whatever the case, it's a very nice touch to honor your guests when your party wraps up.

Last, the majority of the recipes within these pages are extremely user friendly, so that your holiday entertaining is something that you can look forward to with anticipation, instead of with trepidation. Remember that the holidays are truly the most wonderful time of the year to share with friends and family, and this book will definitely help you navigate them, in whatever way you choose to celebrate, with a minimum of fuss. So prepare to deck the halls and party Daisy-style, with a little bit of Latino flair, some sassy dishes, and a whole lot of festive fun!

My daughter, Angela,
preparing the Thanksgiving
turkey, 1998.

My husband, Jerry, preparing to
carve the turkey, 1999.

Family hayride at the Christmas
tree farm. From left to right: David, Marc,
Angela, me, Jerry, and Erik, 2005.

Angela and my son Erik opening gifts, Christmas morning, 2008.

Angela and my son David decorating the Christmas tree, 2008.

Angela celebrating New Year's Eve in Barcelona, 2003.

DAISY'S
HOLIDAY COOKING

CHAPTER ONE

Cozy Festive Fall Dinner

Serves 6

Velvety Cauliflower-Pear Soup

Crispy Potato-Cabrales Wontons
(optional; page 54)

Mushroom-Plantain-Stuffed Chicken Breasts
with Mango-Bacon Gravy

Fenneled-Up Brussels Sprouts

One Cake, Two Ways (Coconut Cream Triple-Layer Cake or
"Deconstructed" *Tres Leches*)

As fall kicks into high gear, I feel the urge to get back into "serious" entertaining. I know the holidays—and the partying with friends and family they bring—are just around the corner. I like to plan a quiet sit-down dinner when my husband, Jerry, and I can chill with a few good friends. They may be friends we don't usually see during the holidays or even those we *do* see but would like to share a quieter evening with before all the hubbub begins.

This is a perfect menu for just such a dinner. The Crispy Potato-Cabrales Wontons offer a lovely contrast to the Velvety Cauliflower-Pear Soup or can be enjoyed as a charming *amuse-bouche* with drinks before your guests sit down at the table. The very special chicken breasts, stuffed with mushrooms and coarsely mashed sweet plantains, are a tour de force—you'll never think of chicken breasts in quite the same way after tasting these. As a closer, the rich coconut layer cake (or the *tres leches* version, if you decide to go that route) manages to pull off homeyness and sophistication at the same time. Virtually everything, with the exception of sautéing the Brussels sprouts and roasting and slicing the chicken, can be done well in advance, meaning you won't miss out on the fun.

Keep this menu in mind for Thanksgiving too. If you are celebrating with just a few people, and a whole turkey seems like too big a deal, maybe America's favorite bird is the answer. That was the case on the first Thanksgiving that Jerry and I spent together as a married couple. Jerry was a medical resident, and my son Erik was a little more than a month old. There was no way that Jerry and I could deal with a whole turkey and the leftovers, so I decided to make a large roast chicken instead. It's one of my happiest Thanksgiving memories, just the four of us: my growing family and that simple roast chicken.

Mushroom-Plantain-Stuffed Chicken Breasts with Mango-Bacon Gravy

MAKES 6 SERVINGS

For Thanksgiving, turkey is the bird of choice. If you're not wild about turkey, or you think your group is too small to fuss with one, or if you're just plain turkeyed out, it may be time to turn your attention to another bird altogether—in this case breast of chicken stuffed with sizzled mushrooms and sweet plantains and sauced with a smoky-sweet pan gravy.

I'll tell you up front that this dish requires some time in the kitchen. I'll also tell you that that time can be spread out over 3 days prior to the dinner. Come showtime, you'll look like a pro as you calmly pull together all your prepared items for a truly special main course. (Not to mention that the gravy gets *better* after a couple of days.)

Whether you're preparing the stuffed chicken breasts or the simpler version that follows, you really need skin-on chicken for this—the crispness of the skin after it's been pan-seared is lovely with the silky gravy and the chunky-chewy plantain mash.

FOR THE STUFFED CHICKEN BREASTS:
Mushroom *Picadillo* (page 13)
Ripe Plantain Mash (page 11)
Three 3½-pound chickens (preferably free-range and/or organic)
Kosher or fine sea salt and freshly ground pepper

FOR THE MANGO-BACON GRAVY:
12 ounces slab bacon, rind removed, cut into ½-inch cubes (about 2 cups)
1 large onion, halved, then cut into thick slices
2 medium carrots, peeled and coarsely chopped
4 stalks celery, trimmed and coarsely chopped
3 cloves garlic, coarsely chopped
¼ cup all-purpose flour
6 cups homemade or store-bought chicken broth
2 sprigs fresh thyme
1 bay leaf
1 teaspoon black peppercorns
1½ cups mango nectar (see Note)
2 tablespoons white wine vinegar

2 tablespoons olive oil
Fenneled-Up Brussels Sprouts (page 14), for serving

Mushroom-Plantain-Stuffed Chicken Breasts with Mango-Bacon Gravy and Fenneled-Up Brussels Sprouts.

1. Make the *picadillo* and the plantain mash. The *picadillo* can be made up to 3 days in advance and the plantains can be made up to 1 day in advance.

Prepare and cut up the chickens:

2. Rinse the giblets and necks and set them all, except for the livers, aside for the gravy. Use the livers for another dish or discard them.

3. For each chicken, feel along the center of the chicken breast to find the thin bone that separates the two breast halves. With a thin-bladed knife, cut along one side of this bone and down to the rib bones. Pull the breast meat away from the center bone—so you can get a better look at what you're doing—and using the tip of the knife, start to separate the breast meat from the rib bones. Keep going like this, following the curve of the rib bones, until you reach the joint where the wing connects to the breastbone. Cut through the skin along the backbone—but not through the skin that connects the breast to the thigh (you'll get to that in a minute). When you reach the point where the wing bone connects to the breastbone, bend the wing behind the chicken to give yourself a very clear view of the joint. Cut through the joint to separate the wing from the breastbone. You now have a skin-on boneless breast (with the wing attached) that is still attached to the thigh by the skin. Slip your fingertip under the skin of the thigh to separate the skin from the meat. Pull back the skin from the leg, leaving the skin attached to the breast. Cut off as much of the skin from the thigh as you can, being sure to leave that skin attached to the skin that covers the breast. Cut off the wing tip and middle joint of the wing, leaving the first joint of the wing attached to the breast. (This is known as a Frenched chicken breast.) You will now have a boneless chicken breast with a fair amount of extra skin (from the thigh) attached along one edge and the first wing joint attached to the other end. Trim any pieces of fat or cartilage from the breast and repeat with the other breast half. When you've finished removing the two breasts, remove the legs by bending them backward to expose the joints that connect the legs to the backbone. Cut through the skin, meat, and those joints to remove the legs. Set the legs and trimmed wing pieces aside for another use. Trim all the fat and skin from the breastbones and backbones of the 3 chickens and, with a heavy knife or a cleaver, whack the bones into manageable pieces. Set the bones aside for the gravy.

Butterfly and stuff the chicken breasts:

4. To butterfly the chicken, start at the wider, thicker long side of each breast and make a horizontal cut almost all the way through the breast, stopping just before cutting through the thin side of the breast. Season both sides of the breasts with salt and pepper.

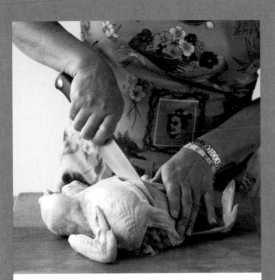

Remove the first breast from the chicken by cutting along one side of the breastbone down to the rib bones.

Cut through the joint that attaches the wing to the breastbone.

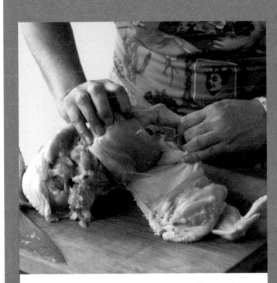

Pull back the skin from the leg, but leave the skin attached to the breast.

To butterfly the boneless chicken breast, make a horizontal cut through the breast starting at the wider, thicker, long side of the breast.

5. Take ¼ cup of the plantain mash and shape it into a more or less even roll about 2 inches long. Repeat to make 5 more rolls and set them aside. Open up one of the butterflied chicken breasts with one of the long sides closest to you. Spread ¼ cup of the mushroom *picadillo* over the surface of the meat, leaving about a ½-inch border all the way around. Place one of the plantain rolls along the edge of the chicken breast closest to you. Roll up the chicken breast, tucking in the ends as you go, to make a neat, compact little bundle with the wing joint protruding from one end. There will be a little skin left on the far side—smooth that into place to cover up the seam and to cover up as much of the breast meat as possible and make an even neater bundle. With the seam side down, tie the stuffed breast at 1-inch intervals with kitchen twine. Do the same with the rest of the breasts, mushroom *picadillo,* and plantain rolls. Pat the stuffed breasts dry with paper towels. The chickens can be boned and seasoned up to 2 days before cooking them, and the breasts can be stuffed up to several hours before. Keep them refrigerated in a covered container.

Make the mango-bacon gravy:

6. Put the bacon cubes in a wide braising pan or casserole and pour in ¼ cup water. Set over high heat and cook until the water is almost evaporated, then reduce the heat to medium-low. *(Starting the bacon with a little water helps pull some of the fat out of the bacon. By the time the water has evaporated, the bacon will be sizzling gently in its own fat.)* Cook until the bacon is lightly browned and the bottom of the pan is shiny with golden bits stuck to it, about 6 minutes. Add the onion, carrots, celery, and garlic and cook, stirring often so the vegetables do not stick and brown, until the onion is softened but not brown, about 10 minutes.

7. Add the reserved chicken bones and giblets and cook, stirring often, until the bones start to brown and the onion is well browned, about 10 minutes. Poke around the bottom of the pan as you stir to make sure the bones and vegetables aren't sticking and burning as they cook. Sprinkle the flour over the bones and vegetables and stir until you can't see any traces of white. Pour in the broth and add the thyme, bay leaf, and peppercorns. Bring to a boil, stirring up the little browned bits that have stuck to the pan. Adjust the heat so the sauce is simmering and stir in the mango nectar and the vinegar. Cook until the sauce is slightly thickened, smooth, and a rich brown, about 45 minutes. Stir occasionally to prevent sticking, especially in the corners of the pan. Strain the gravy through a very fine sieve. The gravy can be held at room temperature for up to 2 hours or refrigerated for up to 3 days. In either case, reheat the gravy over low heat, adding water a spoonful at a time to return it to its original thickness.

Cook the stuffed chicken breasts and assemble the plates:

8. About 35 minutes before you're ready to serve the chicken, preheat the oven to 400°F. When it reaches that temperature, heat the 2 tablespoons olive oil in a large, heavy, ovenproof nonstick skillet over medium-high heat. Be sure the chicken breasts are dry and slide them carefully into the oil. Cook, turning as necessary, until they're beautifully browned on all sides, about 10 minutes. Pop the whole pan into the oven and cook until the chicken is cooked through and the filling is warmed, about 20 minutes. *(The best way to check is to use an instant-read thermometer. The temperature at the very center of the stuffing should reach 150°F.)*

9. Let the chicken breasts rest for about 5 minutes. Meanwhile, cook the prepared Brussels sprouts and make sure the gravy is hot.

10. To serve: Snip the twine off the chicken breasts. Slice the breasts on the diagonal into 4 or 5 slices each. Arrange the slices overlapping along one side of each plate. Spoon some Brussels sprouts onto the other side of the plate. Ladle enough gravy over the sliced chicken to nap it and form a little pool on the plate. Serve immediately.

NOTE: Mango nectar is a pulpy juice extracted from fresh mangoes. It is available fresh in cartons in some Latin markets and health food stores or in bottles, cartons, or cans in many supermarkets.

VARIATION: Pan-Roasted Chicken Breasts with Mango-Bacon Gravy, Mushroom *Picadillo*, and Ripe Plantain Mash

This version of the above recipe uses all the same components—chicken breasts, plantain mash, and mushroom *picadillo*—but presents them differently. Here, a pan-seared chicken breast sits atop a bed of mushroom and is flanked by a chunky plantain mash and sautéed Brussels sprouts.

- Start with 6 Frenched chicken breasts (see Note below). Up to 2 days before serving, season them generously with kosher or fine sea salt and freshly ground pepper. Prepare the Mushroom *Picadillo* and Mango-Bacon Gravy 1 to 2 days in advance. Prep the ingredients for the Fenneled-Up Brussels Sprouts (page 14)—but don't cook them—and make the Ripe Plantain Mash up to several hours before serving. After making the mushrooms and the plantain mash, store them in microwavable containers. When it comes time to assemble the plates, you'll be able to take them right from the refrigerator and into the microwave oven.

- Remove the chicken from the refrigerator about 30 minutes before cooking. About 15 minutes before serving, reheat the gravy in a small, heavy saucepan over very low heat and start cooking the chicken: Heat the 2 tablespoons olive oil in a heavy skillet large enough to hold all the chicken in a single layer over high heat. If necessary, cook the chicken in 2 skillets and increase the amount of oil by about a tablespoon, using about 1½ tablespoons in each. Lay the chicken breasts in the skillet(s), skin side down (watch for splattering!), and cook just until they start to color. Reduce the heat to medium and cook until the skin side is a deep golden brown and crisp, about 4 minutes. Flip the breast and cook until the meat side is golden brown and the chicken is cooked through in the thickest part (where the wing bone meets the breast), about 5 minutes. The best way to tell if the chicken is done is to test the thickest part close to the wing bone with an instant-read thermometer. The temperature should be at least 155°. Remove the chicken to a cutting board and let stand while you get the rest of the meal ready.

- Prepare the Brussels sprouts and remove the pan from the heat. Warm the mushrooms and the plantain mash in the microwave oven until heated through, about 2½ to 3 minutes for each. Spoon about ¼ cup of the mushrooms onto the center of each dinner plate. Top with a chicken breast, skin side up. Spoon some of the plantain mash to one side of the chicken and some of the sprouts to the other. Ladle enough of the gravy over the chicken to coat the chicken and make little pools of gravy on the plate. Pass the remaining gravy at the table.

NOTE: A Frenched chicken breast is a single, skin-on boneless breast with the first wing joint attached. The butcher department of many supermarkets will be able to prepare them for you. Ask to keep the breastbones left over after boning the breasts—you'll need them for the gravy. If you can't get the breastbones, buy 1½ pounds chicken necks, wings, and/or giblets (no livers) to use in the gravy.

Ripe Plaintain Mash
(NOT QUITE *MOFONGO*)

MAKES ABOUT 4 CUPS

Maybe I should start by explaining what *mofongo* is before I tell you why this isn't quite it. *Mofongo* starts with green (i.e., unripe, starchy) plantains that are cooked and then mashed with garlic, pork cracklings, and the fat rendered from making the cracklings, to a coarse and crunchy mash. Diet food, it isn't—delicious, it is.

When I first made this simple mixture of ripened plantains as a filling for the chicken breasts on page 5, I boiled the plantains until fully tender and mashed them until smooth. Then I tried a version with slightly-less-than-tender plantains mashed coarsely, like *mofongo,* and found I liked that texture much better.

If your bird is a whole turkey, serve this as an unexpected side dish, along with the usual yams and cranberry sauce. Or whip up a batch of this not-quite-*mofongo* and serve alongside fried eggs, chorizo, and pickled onion (see page 34) for breakfast on a chilly autumn morning.

3 medium plantains (see Note), peeled and cut into 3 pieces each
Kosher or fine sea salt

2 tablespoons unsalted butter
Freshly ground pepper

1. Put the plantains in a medium saucepan and add enough water to cover by a couple of inches. Add a rounded teaspoon of salt and bring to a boil over high heat. Adjust the heat so the water is simmering. Cook until you can pierce the plantains easily with a paring knife, but there is still some texture, about 6 minutes.
2. Drain the plantains and let them air-dry for a few minutes. Put them in a food processor along with the butter and 2 tablespoons water. Process, using very quick on-off pulses, just until the smaller pieces of plantain are starting to become smooth. The texture should be very coarse and you should still be able to see pieces of plantain in the mash. Scrape into a bowl and season to taste with salt and pepper. Serve hot.

NOTE: The skin of the plantains should be mostly black with some speckling of yellow. The flesh should have some give when you press it with your thumb.

Velvety Cauliflower-Pear Soup

(SEE PHOTO, PAGE 82)

MAKES ABOUT 8 CUPS (6 FIRST-COURSE SERVINGS PLUS LEFTOVERS)

Pairing cauliflower with ripe, sweet pears may seem an odd combination until you think about the many happy marriages between other members of the cabbage family and their "sweeties": coleslaw sweetened with everything from plain sugar to pineapple, and the sweet-sour sauces that accompany stuffed cabbages in eastern European cooking. Here, Bartlett pears add texture and a mild sweetness to an otherwise very simple cauliflower soup.

Whether you're making your own vegetable broth or buying it, the color will vary from batch to batch or brand to brand. Avoid dark or orangey broth if possible—the color of the finished soup should be a pale yellow.

Crispy Potato-Cabrales Wontons (optional; page 54)

1 medium head cauliflower

2 tablespoons olive oil

1 small onion, cut into fine dice (about 1 cup)

4 cups homemade or store-bought vegetable broth

2 Bartlett pears, peeled, cut into quarters, and cored

Kosher or fine sea salt

¾ cup evaporated milk

Juice of ½ lemon, or to taste

1. Make the wontons, if using, and freeze or refrigerate until you serve the soup. If frozen, remove them to the refrigerator about 30 minutes before your guests arrive.
2. Trim off all the green leaves from the cauliflower. Cut the head in half and cut out the thick center stem. Cut the cauliflower into large florets; you will have about 12 cups of cut-up cauliflower.
3. Heat the oil in a 5-quart pot over medium heat. Add the onion and cook, stirring occasionally, until softened, about 5 minutes. Add the cauliflower and toss to coat with the seasoned oil. Pour in the broth and add the pears. Season lightly with salt, cover the pot, and bring to a boil. Adjust the heat so the liquid is at a slow boil and cook until the pears and cauliflower are tender, 15 to 20 minutes.

4. Working in batches, blend the soup until smooth. To avoid splattering, either let the soup cool to tepid or work in very small batches and use a folded-up kitchen towel to clamp the lid to the blender while the machine is running. Pour each batch into a clean pot as you finish. Stir in the evaporated milk and lemon juice and season with salt if necessary. The soup may be reheated right away, refrigerated for up to 3 days, or frozen for up to 2 months.

5. While the soup is reheating, fry the wontons (see page 55), if using.

6. Ladle the hot soup into warm serving bowls. Serve 2 or 3 wontons per person on the side and encourage people to dip the crispy wontons in the soup before nibbling. Serve right away.

LUSCIOUS LEFTOVERS: Don't be tempted to make just the amount of wontons you need for this soup. Making the wontons is easy and they freeze beautifully. Make the full batch and keep a stash in the freezer ready to fry up for drop-in guests or for an accompaniment to other smooth-textured soups in search of a little crunch.

Mushroom *Picadillo*

MAKES ABOUT 1½ LOOSELY PACKED CUPS

To the French, this is known as *duxelles*—a simple mixture of sautéed mushrooms and shallots. In my world, it reminds me of *picadillo*, the well-seasoned ground beef (or pork) dish that is eaten on its own or used as a filling for turnovers, vegetables, or croquettes.

If you don't mind the chopping, triple the recipe (cooking each batch separately), freeze two-thirds, and you'll be all set for a batch of Mushroom Croquettes (page 59) and a whole lot more: Use these mushrooms to liven up a pot of soup or stew or as an *empanadita* filling (see page 63 for *empanadita*-making instructions), or stir a few spoonfuls into your next pan of simple white rice.

One 14-ounce package white mushrooms
2 tablespoons olive oil
2 small shallots, finely chopped

Kosher or fine sea salt and freshly ground pepper
Lemon juice

1. Wipe the mushroom caps clean with a damp paper towel. Cut the caps in half and then slice them thin. Chop them fine by rocking your knife back and forth over them, a little mound at a time. You'll have about 8 cups *(This is a labor of love. You may be tempted to chop the mushrooms in a food processor, but that would make them mushy, and you wouldn't end up with the nicely browned, pebbly texture of hand-chopped mushrooms.)*

2. Heat the oil in a large skillet over medium-high heat. Add the shallots and cook, stirring, until they're softened, about 3 minutes. Add the mushrooms and stir until they give up enough liquid to coat the bottom of the pan. Reduce the heat to medium-low and cook until all the liquid has evaporated and the tiny pieces of mushroom are separate, almost fluffy. Season with salt and pepper and enough lemon juice to give it a lively zing. The *picadillo* will keep in the refrigerator for up to 4 days or up to 2 months in the freezer.

Fenneled-Up Brussels Sprouts

(SEE PHOTO, PAGE 4)

MAKES 6 SERVINGS

We all know that overcooking Brussels sprouts is a pretty mean thing to do to them. I'm making a 180-degree turn and suggesting that you cook your sprouts for a matter of minutes. Slicing them thin makes this possible. Teaming the sprouts up with fennel seeds makes them delicious.

Two 10-ounce containers or 1¼ pounds
loose Brussels sprouts
2 tablespoons olive oil

1 teaspoon fennel seeds
Kosher or fine sea salt and freshly ground
pepper

1. Trim the little stalk off the end of each sprout. Cut the sprouts in half, then cut the halves—flat side down, so they stay steady—into thin (about ⅛-inch) shreds. You will have about 7 cups shredded sprouts. The sprouts may be shredded up to several hours before cooking them.

2. Heat the oil in a large, heavy skillet over medium-high heat. Add the fennel seeds and

cook just until they smell wonderful and are sizzling. Stir in the sprouts and cook, tossing and stirring the sprouts, until they are wilted down, bright green, and softened, about 4 minutes. Pull the pan from the heat and season with salt and pepper to taste. Serve hot.

One Cake, Two Ways

(COCONUT CREAM TRIPLE-LAYER CAKE OR "DECONSTRUCTED" *TRES LECHES*)

MAKES 12 SERVINGS OF LAYER CAKE OR 8 SERVINGS OF *TRES LECHES*

The pineapple in this very simple sponge cake keeps the cake nice and moist whether you decide to use the cake for a triple-layer cake frosted and decorated with coconut or to make individual servings of the Latin American classic *tres leches*. Either way you cut it, frost it, dress it, or serve it, this cake is a keeper.

FOR THE PINEAPPLE SPONGE CAKE:
Vegetable oil cooking spray
2 cups all-purpose flour
1½ tablespoons baking powder
1 teaspoon kosher or fine sea salt
8 tablespoons (1 stick) unsalted butter, softened
1¼ cups granulated sugar
2 large eggs
½ cup evaporated milk
1 teaspoon vanilla extract
One 8-ounce can crushed pineapple, well drained

IF MAKING THE COCONUT LAYER CAKE:
1½ cups shredded sweetened coconut
8 ounces cream cheese, softened
¾ cup confectioners' sugar
¼ cup cream of coconut (Coco López or other)
1 cup heavy cream, chilled

IF MAKING THE *TRES LECHES* VARIATION:
2 cups heavy cream
1½ cups evaporated milk
¾ cup sweetened condensed milk
3 cups sliced hulled strawberries or mixed berries
1 tablespoon confectioners' sugar

Make the pineapple sponge cake:

1. Set a rack in the center of the oven and preheat the oven to 350°F. Spray a half sheet pan (18 by 13 inches) with cooking spray. Cut a piece of parchment paper to fit the bottom of the pan and spray the paper.

2. Sift the flour, baking powder, and salt together into a bowl. With an electric mixer, beat the butter and sugar until light in color and fluffy, 4 to 5 minutes. Beat in the eggs one at a time. Stop after each addition to scrape down the sides of the bowl. Beat in the evaporated milk and vanilla. Fold the flour mixture into the wet ingredients just until the two are blended—don't overmix. Scatter the pineapple over the batter and fold in.

3. Scrape the batter into the prepared pan and spread it into an even layer. Bake until the center of the cake springs back when poked and the edges are golden brown and start to pull away from the sides of the pan, about 20 minutes. Let the cake cool completely.

If making the coconut layer cake, while the cake is cooling, make the topping and frosting:

4. Toast the coconut in a large skillet over medium-low heat until it is lightly browned (see Note). Remove from the heat and let cool.

5. Beat the cream cheese and confectioners' sugar in a medium bowl until very light and fluffy. Whisk in the cream of coconut. In a separate bowl (a chilled metal or glass bowl and chilled beaters will help), beat the heavy cream until it holds stiff peaks when the beaters are lifted from it. Fold the whipped cream into the cream cheese mixture with a rubber spatula.

Assemble the layer cake:

6. Slide the cake, still on the parchment, out of the pan and onto a cutting board. Cut the cake in thirds crosswise making 3 rectangular layers each about 12 by 6 inches. Center one of the layers on a serving platter. Spread about one-fourth of the frosting over the layer, spreading it all the way to the edges. Repeat with another cake layer and about one-third of the remaining frosting. Center the last layer on top and spread the top and sides of the cake with all the remaining frosting. Make sure the toasted coconut is completely cool and, working with a small handful of the coconut at a time, press it gently onto the top and sides of the cake.

7. Chill the cake for at least 1 hour or up to 1 day before serving. If holding for longer than

One Cake, Two Ways (Coconut Cream Triple-Layer Cake version).

an hour, chill the cake uncovered (to give the frosting a chance to set up) for 1 hour, then cover gently with plastic wrap. Let the cake stand at room temperature for about 30 minutes before serving. Cut into 1-inch slices using a serrated knife and a gentle back-and-forth sawing motion.

If making the *tres leches* variation:

8. After taking the cake out of the oven, make the *tres leches* mix: Stir together 1 cup of the heavy cream, the evaporated milk, and the sweetened condensed milk in a bowl. Poke the cake all over the surface with a dinner fork and brush about ½ cup of the *tres leches* mix over the top. Let the cake cool completely and refrigerate the remaining *tres leches* mix.

9. About an hour before serving the dessert, toss the berries and confectioners' sugar in a small bowl and let stand at room temperature. Using a 3-inch round biscuit cutter or decorative cutter (star, flower, etc.), cut the pineapple cake into rounds or shapes (you'll need 2 per serving).

10. To serve: Whip the remaining 1 cup cream (a chilled bowl and chilled beaters help) until it holds soft peaks when the beaters are lifted from it. Put one of the cake rounds in each of 6 shallow bowls (or work with as many bowls as your space allows). Pour about 2 tablespoons of the *tres leches* mix over the cake and top with ½ cup of the berries and some of their juice. Dollop some of the whipped cream over the berries and top with a second cake round. Pour another 2 tablespoons of the *tres leches* mix over the top layer. Pass any remaining *tres leches* mix and whipped cream separately.

NOTE: Toasting the coconut in a pan on the stove top gives you coconut with varying shades of toastiness; some of the shreds will be deep brown and some pale ivory, with the rest somewhere in between. I like this effect, but if you're striving for perfectly golden brown toasted coconut, toast it in the oven instead: Spread the coconut out in an even layer in a rimmed baking pan and toast in a 350°F oven, stirring a few times, from 10 to 15 minutes, depending on the shade of golden brown you like. But remember, whichever method you use, sweetened coconut contains quite a bit of sugar, and once it starts to brown, it really takes off.

Preparation Schedule

Up to 1 month before the dinner:
- Make the soup (if freezing).
- Make and freeze the wontons (if using).

Up to 3 days before the dinner:
- Make the mushroom *picadillo*.
- Make the gravy.

Up to 2 days before the dinner:
- Bone the chickens and butterfly the breasts.
- Make the soup (if not freezing).

Up to 1 day before the dinner:
- Make the pineapple sheet cake.
- Make the frosting, toast the coconut, and assemble the cake (if serving the coconut layer cake).
- Make the *tres leches* mix (if serving the *tres leches* variation of the cake).
- Make the plantain mash.

Up to several hours before the dinner:
- Shred the Brussels sprouts (but don't cook them yet!).
- Stuff and tie the chicken breasts.
- Prep the fruit and cut the cake shapes for *tres leches* (if serving).

Just before guests arrive:
- Pan-sear the chicken and preheat the oven (but don't put the chicken in yet!).
- Remove the wontons (if serving) to the refrigerator.

As guests arrive:
- Warm the soup and fry the wontons (if serving).
- Take the coconut layer cake (if serving) out of the refrigerator to bring to room temperature.

After clearing the soup plates:
- Pop the chicken breasts into the oven and while they're baking:
  - Warm the gravy.
  - Cook the Brussels sprouts.
- Slice and plate the chicken.

After clearing the dinner plates:
- Slice and serve the coconut layer cake (if serving) or serve the *tres leches* version.

CHAPTER TWO

Thanksgiving Buffet

Serves 12

Red Snapper *Tiradito* Skewers

~

Coconut and Winter Squash Soup with Toasted Almonds

~

Achiote-Rubbed Roast Turkey with *Manchamanteles*

Corn Bread–*Longaniza* Stuffing

Shrimp-Stuffed Zucchini Cups

Yuca *"Mofongo"* and/or Fenneled-Up Brussels Sprouts (page 14)

~

Flourless Chocolate-Chile Cake

~

Chilean Mulled Red Wine

When I was growing up, our home was the center of the Thanksgiving celebration. *Mami* comes from a large family, so by the time we invited all our aunts, uncles, and cousins, and threw any number of close family friends into the mix, there was quite a crowd. If you have a sizable group of family and friends, a buffet like this one is pretty much the best (and easiest) way to go.

The main event on our Thanksgiving menu was always *pavochon*—an enormous turkey rubbed with an oregano-and-garlic-rich adobo. *Mami* always enlisted my help for grinding the adobo ingredients to a paste in her mortar. I still love *pavochon* (and included recipes for it in my first two books), but I like to switch things up every once in a while and put my own spin on holiday get-togethers.

While I was traveling in Mexico with my husband and children, my son David fell in love with a dish called *cochinita pil bil,* an achiote-rubbed piece of pork that is wrapped in banana leaves and roasted in a clay pit. I've also eaten chicken prepared in this manner, and so the leap to turkey (at least in my head) was not a big one. Season your turkey with the achiote rub (see page 26) a day or two beforehand, so the flavors have a chance to work their way into the meat. Paired with a fruity mole with warm ancho chile notes, this turkey is a festive addition to your autumnal celebration. The bacony yuca (which my son Erik requests every year!) and the stuffed zucchini cups are sure to become favorites at your table any time of year.

Red Snapper *Tiradito* Skewers

MAKES 16 SKEWERS

Tiradito—a Peruvian take on ceviche—is raw fish or shellfish marinated in citrus for minutes or just drizzled or brushed with citrus right before serving. It is closer to sashimi than it is to the fully "cooked" ceviche of other Latin American countries, such as Mexico and Ecuador. (Most likely, it's the influence of Peru's many Japanese immigrants!) The *tiradito* I tasted in Peru was dressed at the last minute with citrus juice, olive oil, and salt and served with a side of sweet potatoes, roasted corn, red onions, and/or other vegetables. My take on the theme features lightly marinated (half-"cooked") strips of snapper and is sort of a mini *tiradito* plate on a skewer—perfect for cocktail parties. It goes without saying that whichever type of fish you choose, it should be the freshest possible.

Four 3-ounce red snapper fillets (see
  Notes)
Juice of 2 lemons
Juice of 2 limes
1½ teaspoons kosher or fine sea salt, plus
  more for seasoning the dressing
2 oranges or blood oranges, or 1 pink or
  yellow grapefruit

16 small grape tomatoes
16 kalamata olives, pitted (or pitted
  olives of your choice)
3 tablespoons good olive oil
Freshly ground pepper

1. Cut each of the fillets into strips about 4 inches long by ¾ inch wide. (You may have a few more than you need—a snack for the cook!) Size up the fillets before you start slicing; based on the size and shape of the fillets, you may want to slice them crosswise, lengthwise, or on an angle. Stir the lemon and lime juices and the 1½ teaspoons salt together in a small bowl until the salt has dissolved. Add the snapper strips and turn them gently so they are covered in juice. Cover and refrigerate for 2 hours.

2. Meanwhile, cut off the peel and pith from the citrus of your choice, removing all of the pith but taking as little of the fruit as possible. Hold the fruit over a bowl and free the segments from between the membranes with a paring knife, letting the segments fall into the bowl as you go. Squeeze all of the juice out of the membranes and into the bowl. Remove

the seeds, if any, from the segments, and cut very large grapefruit segments (if using) in half crosswise. Drain the juice from the segments and set the juice and segments aside separately.

3. Make the skewers: Drain the snapper strips and discard the marinade. Thread one of the citrus segments onto a plain or decorative 6-inch (or so) bamboo skewer. Poke the tip of the skewer through the end of one of the snapper strips. Follow with a grape tomato, then fold the snapper over the tomato and gently nudge the tomato and snapper down the skewer. Poke the tip through an olive and fold the last of the snapper strip over the olive and onto the tip of the skewer to finish it up. Repeat with the remaining skewers, fruit, snapper, tomatoes, and olives. Arrange the skewers, in a single layer if possible, on a baking sheet or flat plate, cover with plastic wrap, and refrigerate. The skewers can be assembled up to several hours before serving them, but no more.

4. Make the dressing: Whisk the reserved citrus juice and olive oil together in a small bowl. Season with salt and pepper to taste.

5. To serve: Whisk the dressing well to blend it thoroughly. Brush the skewers with the dressing and serve immediately.

NOTES

- Small fillets—about 4 ounces each with the skin on and 3 ounces without—will yield the right size strips of snapper for threading onto the skewers. If you're starting with a whole snapper and asking your fishmonger to clean and fillet it for you, ask for a whole snapper that weighs about 1¾ pounds. In either case, have the fishmonger remove the skin and all the little pin bones from the fillets.

- If you prefer, grilled small (about 40 per pound) shrimp or broiled bay scallops may be substituted for the marinated snapper. Use 2 shrimp or scallops per skewer, and brush them with a little of the citrus dressing before cooking. Just before serving, brush the skewers with the remaining citrus dressing. Cook the shrimp or scallops close to party time; they will be better if they haven't been refrigerated.

Coconut and Winter Squash Soup with Toasted Almonds

MAKES 12 BUFFET SERVINGS (ABOUT 8 CUPS)

This soup draws inspiration from pumpkin pie, with its creamy texture and familiar autumn spices, but it's given a tropical punch with coconut milk.

2 tablespoons unsalted butter

3 large shallots, finely diced (about ¼ cup)

8 cups diced (½-inch) peeled and seeded calabaza, sugar pumpkin, or butternut squash (about 4 pounds whole)

2 cups homemade or store-bought chicken broth

½ vanilla bean

1 cinnamon stick

Kosher or fine sea salt and freshly ground pepper (preferably white)

One 13.5-ounce can unsweetened coconut milk

⅓ teaspoon ground cloves

¼ teaspoon ground allspice

Toasted sliced almonds (see Note, page 43)

1. Melt the butter in a 4- to 5-quart soup pot or Dutch oven over medium-low heat. Add the shallots and cook, stirring occasionally, until soft and fragrant, about 4 minutes. Keep the heat low so the shallots don't brown. Add the calabaza and the chicken broth, raise the heat to high, and bring to a boil. Add the vanilla bean and the cinnamon stick and season lightly with salt and pepper. Adjust the heat so the broth is simmering, cover the pot, and cook until the calabaza is very soft, about 20 minutes.

2. Remove the vanilla bean from the soup, split it lengthwise with a paring knife, and scrape the vanilla specks from inside the bean into the pot. Remove and discard the cinnamon stick. Working in batches, blend the soup until very smooth. To avoid splattering, either let the soup cool to tepid or work in very small batches and use a folded-up kitchen towel to clamp the lid to the blender while the machine is running. Pour each batch into a clean pot as you finish. Season with salt and pepper to taste.

3. Whisk in the coconut milk, cloves, and allspice. Heat the soup gently until heated through. The soup can be prepared completely in advance up to 2 days before serving. Refrigerate and bring back to a simmer, stirring, over very low heat before serving. Sprinkle a generous amount of the toasted almonds over each bowl of soup.

Achiote-Rubbed Roast Turkey with *Manchamanteles*

MAKES 12 SERVINGS (PLUS LEFTOVERS)

Pork is overwhelmingly the main course of choice for celebrations in the Latin countries I have visited, including Peru, Mexico, Spain, and, of course, my own Puerto Rico. If pork isn't the main event, then, nine times out of ten, turkey will be. This version of a festive bird comes from Mexico, with a stopover in Puerto Rico. Roasted meats in Mexico are often rubbed with a highly seasoned achiote paste, which gives them a very pronounced flavor and, to my mind, a slightly gritty texture. I prefer to make my own rub with achiote (annatto) oil, a little garlic, and some salt and pepper. The flavor is fairly mild (but delicious!) and doesn't fight with the very flavorful sauce.

Manchamanteles (page 29)
One 12- to 14-pound turkey (preferably
    free-range and/or organic)

FOR THE ACHIOTE RUB:
⅓ cup olive oil
1 tablespoon achiote seeds
4 cloves garlic, peeled
2 tablespoons salt
1 tablespoon cracked black peppercorns

1. Make the *manchamanteles* up to 3 days in advance.
2. Remove the giblets and neck from the turkey. Save them for broth (see Luscious Leftovers). Rinse the turkey inside and out under cold water and drain off as much water as possible. Blot the turkey dry inside and out with a wad of paper towels.

Make the achiote rub and season the turkey:

3. Heat the olive oil and achiote seeds in a small skillet over low heat until the seeds are sizzling and the oil begins to darken. Let the seeds sizzle for 1 minute, then strain the oil into a small heatproof bowl. With a garlic press, press the garlic cloves into the oil. *(Adding*

Achiote-Rubbed Roast Turkey with *Manchamanteles* and Corn Bread–*Longaniza* Stuffing.

the garlic to the hot oil mellows it out a little bit and takes out the "sting.") Stir in the salt and the peppercorns and let the oil cool to room temperature.

4. Loosen the skin over the turkey breast and as much of the legs as you can by working your fingers gently (to avoid tearing the skin) in between the meat and skin. Flip the turkey over and do the same to as much of the skin over the back as you can. Using your fingers, work the achiote rub into the meat under all the loosened skin and inside the cavity of the turkey. Truss the turkey legs with kitchen twine and smear any remaining rub over the turkey skin.

5. Put the turkey, breast side down, on a rack in a roasting pan and refrigerate, uncovered, for up to 2 days (the longer, the better) *(Refrigerating the turkey helps dry the skin, making it crispier after roasting.)*

Cook and serve the turkey:

6. Take the turkey out of the refrigerator and bring to room temperature about 30 minutes before you plan to cook it. Meanwhile, preheat the oven to 425°F.

7. Pour 1 cup water into the roasting pan. Roast the turkey, breast side down, for 45 minutes, then reduce the oven temperature to 375°F. Continue roasting until an instant-read thermometer inserted into the thickest part of the thigh, away from any bone, registers 155°F, about 3¼ hours total cooking time for a 14-pound turkey, or 14 minutes per pound. About 30 minutes before the turkey is done, turn it breast side up on the rack. *(A pair of oven mitts that you're willing to toss into the laundry basket afterward is a good way to turn the turkey. The turkey will continue to cook and the temperature to rise after taking it out of the oven. The final temperature you're looking for is 165°F. The joint where the wing connects to the breastbone is another good place to check the temperature.)* Let the turkey stand for about 30 minutes before carving. Fill a gravy boat with *manchamanteles* and pass it separately.

LUSCIOUS LEFTOVERS: Of course, leftover turkey is half the reason people love Thanksgiving!

- Prepare a Latin version of the classic American day-after-Thanksgiving sandwich filled with turkey, cranberry sauce, gravy, and stuffing by piling sliced turkey and corn bread stuffing into a split length of soft Italian bread. Slather the bread with leftover *manchamanteles*.

- Or substitute sliced turkey for the smoked turkey called for in the panini on page 80.

Manchamanteles (SEE PHOTO, PAGE 27)

(CHILE-FRUIT MOLE)

MAKES ABOUT 7 CUPS (ENOUGH TO SERVE WITH THE ROAST TURKEY ON PAGE 26 AND PROVIDE GENEROUS—AND I MEAN GENEROUS!—LEFTOVERS)

This type of mole, *manchamanteles* (or "tablecloth-stainer"), is so named for the vibrant color contributed by the chiles and fruit—and the mess that people make digging into the finished dish! The rich fruit flavor is a natural with turkey—think cranberry sauce—and any mole makes a great braising sauce for beef short ribs, pork ribs, or the country-style spareribs on page 103— hence the built-in leftovers.

2 ripe medium plum tomatoes (about 8 ounces)

3 tablespoons olive oil

1 large white onion (about 1¼ pounds), halved, then cut into thin slices (about 4 cups)

1 teaspoon dried oregano

½ teaspoon ground cumin

½ cup ancho chile paste (see Note)

6 cups homemade or store-bought chicken broth, or as needed

One 20-ounce can crushed pineapple, with juice

1 mango, peeled, pitted, and cut into ¼-inch dice (about 1½ cups)

4 ounces dried apricots, cut into ¼ inch dice (about ⅔ cup)

1 teaspoon ground cinnamon

¼ teaspoon ground cloves

¼ teaspoon ground allspice

¼ teaspoon ground ginger

¼ teaspoon freshly ground pepper

Kosher or fine sea salt

1. Core the tomatoes and cut them in half lengthwise. Heat a small, heavy skillet (preferably cast iron) over medium-high heat until very hot. Add the tomatoes, skin side down, and cook, turning once, until charred on most of both sides, about 8 minutes. Set them aside.

2. Heat the oil in a large, deep skillet over medium-high heat. Add the onion and cook, stirring often, until it just begins to take on some color, about 8 minutes. Add the oregano and continue cooking until the onion is lightly browned, about 3 minutes. Stir in the cumin, then

the ancho paste. Keep stirring and cooking until the onion is coated with the chile paste. Stir in the 6 cups broth and heat to boiling, then slip in the charred tomatoes. Adjust the heat so the sauce is simmering and cook until the onion is very tender, about 20 minutes.

3. Working in batches, blend the sauce base until smooth. To avoid splattering, either cool the sauce to tepid or work in very small batches and use a folded-up kitchen towel to clamp the lid to the blender while it's running. Rinse out the skillet.

4. Return the sauce base to the skillet. Stir in the pineapple with its juice, the mango, apricots, cinnamon, cloves, allspice, ginger, and pepper. Season lightly with salt and bring to a boil, then adjust the heat so the sauce is simmering. Cook until the sauce is slightly thickened (enough to coat a spoon) and takes on a nice shine, about 20 minutes. If the sauce becomes too thick, add small amounts of broth as necessary. The sauce may be prepared up to 3 days in advance and refrigerated.

NOTE: Ancho chile paste is traditionally made by toasting ancho chiles (which are dried poblano peppers) until softened, seeding them, and pureeing the chiles until very smooth. The new tradition in my kitchen is to order ancho paste online: An excellent ancho paste (and pastes made from other chiles) is available online from Purcell Mountain Farms through their Web site (www.purcellmountainfarms.com). Alternatively, substitute ancho chiles for the paste: Lightly toast 6 to 8 ancho chiles in a heavy skillet over medium-low heat just until they change color and smell wonderful, about 1 minute per side. When the chiles are cool enough to handle, pull out the stems and tap out the seeds. Put the toasted chiles in a large bowl and pour in enough hot water to cover them. Weight them with a plate to keep them submerged and soak them until softened, about 20 minutes. Drain them thoroughly, tear them into large pieces, and put them in a blender jar. Blend, adding just enough fresh water to make a very coarse puree. Any seeds and skins you may have missed will be strained out of the sauce before adding the fruit. Anchos are not particularly fiery, but if you are sensitive to chiles, you may want to put on a pair of disposable latex gloves when working with them.

LUSCIOUS LEFTOVERS: Pick over the turkey and remove all the meat from the bones—even the nooks and crannies. Pick over the meat to remove pieces of fat, skin, or gristle and shred the meat coarsely. Put the meat in a saucepan and spoon in enough of the leftover *manchamanteles* to coat the turkey generously. Warm over low heat until heated through. Serve with rice or use as a filling for soft flour or corn tortillas, crisp corn tacos, or enchiladas. For any of the above, whip up a batch of Quick-Pickled Onion (page 34) and pass a dish of it separately.

Corn Bread–*Longaniza* Stuffing

(SEE PHOTO, PAGE 27)

MAKES 12 SERVINGS

This is a riff on a stuffing that my father used to make for his brothers in the FDNY. My mother, who grew up in Puerto Rico, didn't know from stuffing, so she turned it into something more familiar with the addition of chorizo or *longaniza* sausage and spiced it up, Connie style.

This version is left simple deliberately because it is being served alongside the very complex flavors of the *Manchamanteles* (page 29). If you're serving this stuffing with a more traditional turkey, feel free to add fresh fruits like apples or dried fruits like mangoes, figs, or apricots, or another vegetable, like finely diced jicama or chayote, along with the onion, celery, and carrots.

1 tablespoon olive oil, plus more for the
  baking dish
10 ounces *longaniza* sausage (see Note)
1 large white onion (about 14 ounces),
  diced (about 2½ cups)
5 stalks celery, trimmed and diced (about
  2 cups)

1 cup grated peeled carrots
One 16-ounce bag corn bread stuffing
2½ cups homemade or store-bought
  chicken broth
Kosher or fine sea salt and freshly ground
  pepper

1. Preheat the oven to 350°F. Lightly grease a 13 by 9-inch baking dish with olive oil and set it aside.

2. Poke the *longaniza* all over with a fork. Heat the 1 tablespoon oil in a very large skillet over medium heat. Add the sausage and cook, turning once, until the sausage is well browned and no trace of pink remains in the center, about 8 minutes. Remove the sausage to a paper towel–lined plate and drain.

3. Pour off all but 2 tablespoons of the fat from the pan and return the pan to medium heat. Add the onion, celery, and carrots. Cook, stirring often, until the vegetables are softened but not brown, about 10 minutes.

4. Meanwhile, cut the sausage into ¼-inch slices. Stir the slices into the pan with the vegetables. Scrape the sausage mix into the prepared baking dish. Add the stuffing mix and

toss with the sausage and vegetables. Drizzle the broth over everything, tossing as you do so. Season with salt and pepper to taste. The packaged stuffing can be salty; be careful.

5. Cover the baking dish with a sheet of parchment paper, then a sheet of aluminum foil, crimping the foil along the edges of the dish to seal it good and tight. The stuffing can be made to this point up to 2 days in advance and refrigerated. Bake for 30 minutes (about 35 minutes for refrigerated stuffing) and serve right from the dish.

NOTE: *Longaniza* is a fresh (i.e., not smoked or cooked) pork sausage seasoned with garlic and spices. You will find *longaniza* sweet and hot, just like its Italian counterpart, which you can use if you can't find *longaniza*.

Shrimp-Stuffed Zucchini Cups

MAKES 12 SERVINGS

Known variously as *zapallitos* (Peru) and *calabazines* (Puerto Rico and Mexico), these are often seen as a side dish, but they can do double duty as a first course for a sit-down dinner or as a nibble, passed warm from the oven to accompany drinks before the meal.

FOR THE ZUCCHINI CUPS:
4 medium zucchini (about 6 ounces each)
Olive oil
Kosher or fine sea salt and freshly ground
    pepper

FOR THE FILLING:
2 tablespoons unsalted butter
3 tablespoons all-purpose flour
1 cup milk

2 ripe medium plum tomatoes (about
    8 ounces), peeled, seeded, and
    chopped (see Daisy Does, opposite)
1 tablespoon *ají amarillo* puree
1 pound small shrimp (about 40 per
    pound), peeled, deveined, and cut
    crosswise into 4 pieces
1 tablespoon chopped fresh cilantro

¼ cup freshly grated Parmesan cheese

Make the zucchini cups:

1. Preheat the oven to 375°F.
2. Top and tail the zucchini, then cut them crosswise into 1½-inch lengths. With a melon baller or an espresso spoon, hollow out the zucchini pieces to make little cups to hold the filling: Leave about ½ inch of flesh attached to the bottom of each cup and about ¼ inch along the sides.
3. Brush the zucchini cups all over with olive oil and season them lightly with salt and pepper. Stand them, hollow side up, on a baking sheet and bake until softened but not at all mushy, about 25 minutes. The zucchini can be prepared and baked up to 1 day in advance. Refrigerate the cups until needed.

Make the filling:

4. Melt the butter in a medium saucepan over medium heat. Stir in the flour and whisk until bubbly and smooth. Cook for 2 minutes, whisking constantly and making sure the roux doesn't brown at all. Drizzle in the milk and bring to a simmer, whisking constantly. Cook until the sauce is thickened and smooth, 4 to 5 minutes. Stir in the tomatoes and *ají amarillo* puree, whisk until blended, then fold in the shrimp. Cook, stirring often, just until the shrimp are cooked through, about 4 minutes. Fold in the cilantro. The filling can be made up to 1 day in advance. Let cool to room temperature and refrigerate. Fill the zucchini cups no more than 4 hours before baking.
5. If necessary, reheat the oven to 375°F and spoon the filling into the zucchini cups, filling them to just barely over the top edge. Sprinkle a small amount of the cheese over the filling. Bake until the filling is heated through and the cheese is just starting to brown, about 10 minutes for freshly stuffed cups or about 15 minutes for zucchini and filling that were refrigerated. Serve hot.

DAISY DOES: PEELED AND SEEDED TOMATOES

Bring a large pot of water to a boil. Core the tomatoes and cut an X in the opposite end. Slip the tomatoes into the boiling water and leave them until the skin around the X starts to loosen, 30 to 60 seconds. When the skin loosens, scoop the tomatoes into a bowl of ice water. When they're cool enough to handle, slip off the skins. To seed, cut plum tomatoes in half lengthwise and round tomatoes in half along the "equator." Scoop out and discard the seeds.

Yuca "Mofongo"

MAKES 12 GENEROUS SERVINGS

Anywhere you go now in Puerto Rico, *mofongo* (see page 11) made with yuca (in place of the traditional green plantains) is all the rage. This version is not as crispy-crunchy as traditional *mofongo*—this is more like a chunky mash of yuca laced with bacon and tart pickled red onion. Texture is everything, so be sure not to overcook the yuca. After mixing, this should be a very delicious combination of creamy and chunky.

Pickled red onions are worth making on their own. Try them on sandwiches, tucked into tacos, stirred into soups to add a nice briny note, or as a side with grilled and roasted meats and poultry.

FOR THE QUICK-PICKLED ONION:

1 medium red onion, halved, then cut into
⅛-inch slices
3 tablespoons cider vinegar
1 tablespoon olive oil

FOR THE YUCA:

5 medium yuca (about 4½ pounds) or four
16-ounce bags frozen yuca, defrosted
12 ounces slab bacon, rind removed, cut
into ½-inch cubes (about 2 cups)
Kosher or fine sea salt

Make the pickled onion:

1. Put the onion in a medium skillet. Add the vinegar, olive oil, and 2 tablespoons water. Bring to a boil over medium heat and cook, stirring constantly, just until the liquid has evaporated and the onion starts to sizzle. Pull the pan from the heat immediately—do not let the onion brown even a little. The onion can be made up to 1 day in advance and refrigerated.

Prepare the yuca ingredients:

2. If using fresh yuca, peel it and cut it crosswise into 4-inch lengths. Cut each piece into quarters lengthwise. If using frozen yuca, which has already been peeled and cut into manageable lengths, simply cut the pieces into quarters lengthwise. Find the thin woody "cord" that runs more or less down the center of each yuca and pry it out with the tip of

a paring knife. This may take a little digging. Cut the yuca into ½-inch dice. The yuca may be prepared up to 4 hours before cooking; put it in a bowl large enough to hold it comfortably, cover with cold water, and refrigerate until ready to cook.

3. Render the bacon: Put the bacon in a medium skillet with ¼ cup water. Cook over medium-high heat until the water has evaporated and the bacon starts to sizzle. Reduce the heat to medium and continue cooking until the bacon is well browned and crisp, about 10 minutes. Remove the bacon with a slotted spoon and drain on a paper towel–lined plate. Discard the bacon fat or save it for another dish. The bacon can be cooked early in the day and left at room temperature. (Don't refrigerate.)

4. About 45 minutes before serving the yuca, pour a couple of inches of water into the bottom of a steamer. Bring to a boil, then adjust the heat so the water is boiling gently. Steam the yuca until it is tender and translucent (but not mushy) when poked with a paring knife—start checking after 20 minutes.

5. Transfer the yuca to a serving bowl. Add the bacon and onion and toss just until mixed and some of the yuca is creamy. Season with salt and serve immediately.

LUSCIOUS LEFTOVERS: You'll never regain the creamy-chunky texture of freshly made yuca *mofongo* no matter how hard you try (that's why it's so important to serve this the second it's made). But you can turn it into delicious little fritters: Round 2 tablespoons of leftover yuca *mofongo* between your palms into little balls. Bread them and fry them as you would the Mushroom Croquettes on page 59.

Flourless Chocolate-Chile Cake

MAKE 12 SERVINGS

Mayordomo chocolate is an Oaxacan specialty sold in many markets all over Mexico. Flavored with cinnamon, almonds, and/or vanilla, it is used throughout Oaxaca in hot chocolate, in desserts, and as an ingredient in one of Oaxaca's famed "seven moles." In addition to their chocolate, freshly made hot chocolate, and cocoa beans, the Mayordomo stores feature huge blocks of "mole," not the finished sauce, but a highly seasoned sauce base made with spices, chocolate (of course!), and chiles. I discovered during my trip that Oaxacan cooks buy a chunk of this "mole" and use it to season the mole sauces they make at home.

After my return, I ran into a premium ice cream brand's take on the chocolate-chile theme: Mayan chocolate ice cream. Apparently the pairing of chocolate and chiles wasn't just for savory dishes! So the wheels started turning and I decided to test out a flourless chocolate cake tinged with chile. Here are the results:

1 cup brewed espresso	12 ounces semisweet chocolate
1 cup packed dark brown sugar	4 ounces unsweetened chocolate
3 cinnamon sticks	8 large eggs, beaten
12 ounces (3 sticks) unsalted butter, cubed	Cinnamon ice cream and raspberries, for
1 teaspoon cayenne pepper	serving

1. Preheat the oven to 375°F.
2. Prepare a 9-inch springform pan: Cut a circle of parchment paper the size of the removable bottom of the pan. Fit the parchment circle into the bottom of the pan. Tear off an 18-inch length of aluminum foil. Center the pan over the sheet of foil and crumple and crimp the foil tightly all around the sides of the pan. (The foil will prevent water from seeping into the pan during baking.) Set the pan aside.
3. In a medium saucepan, bring the espresso, brown sugar, and cinnamon sticks to a simmer over very low heat. Turn the heat to the lowest setting and steep until the syrup is very fragrant, about 20 minutes. Remove the cinnamon sticks. Stir in the butter until melted and then stir in the cayenne pepper. Set aside.
4. Pulse the chocolate in the food processor until coarsely chopped. Transfer to a deep bowl.

Pour in the warm coffee syrup and whisk until the chocolate is completely melted. Whisk in the beaten eggs until completely blended.

5. Scrape the batter into the prepared springform pan. Set the pan in a large, deep ovenproof skillet or a roasting pan and set on the oven rack. Pour in enough hot water to come halfway up the sides of the springform pan. Bake until the center is set and barely wiggles when you shake the cake pan gently, 50 to 60 minutes.

6. Remove the cake from the water bath. Let the water bath cool before removing it from the oven. Let the cake cool to room temperature. Remove the foil and chill the cake in its pan for at least 8 hours. Remove to room temperature about 30 minutes before serving. Run a wet knife around the sides of the pan, then pop the spring to release. Place a platter on top of the cake and flip the pan over. Remove the bottom of the pan, and peel off the parchment. *(To cut neat slices of the cake, dip the knife in hot water before and wipe it clean after cutting each slice.)* Serve with cinnamon ice cream and raspberries.

Chilean Mulled Red Wine

(*VINO NAVEGADO*)

MAKES 10 SERVINGS (CAN BE EASILY DOUBLED)

3 cinnamon sticks

1 tablespoon whole cloves

One 1.5-liter bottle dry red wine (about
   6½ cups)

½ cup sugar, or to taste

2 juicy oranges

1. Tie the cinnamon and cloves securely in a large square of cheesecloth. Pour the wine into a heavy nonreactive saucepan. Add the ½ cup sugar and the bundle of spices and bring just to a boil over low heat, stirring to help dissolve the sugar.

2. Meanwhile, cut 1½ of the oranges into thin slices and pick out the seeds. Add the orange slices to the simmering wine, squeeze in the juice from the remaining half orange, and return just to a simmer. Be careful not to boil the wine, especially after adding the orange, as it may become bitter. Serve hot in mugs or heatproof glasses.

Preparation Schedule

Up to 2 days before the buffet:
- Make the soup.
- Make the achiote rub and season the turkey.
- Make the *manchamanteles*.
- Make the stuffing. (Don't bake it yet!)

Up to 1 day before the buffet:
- Make the shrimp filling for the zucchini cups.
- Prep the zucchini cups.
- Bake the chocolate-chile cake.
- Make the pickled onions.

Up to 8 hours before the buffet:
- Toast the almonds for the soup.
- Roast the zucchini cups and let cool.
- Shred the sprouts (if serving, but don't cook them yet!).

About 4 hours before the buffet:
- Prep the *mofongo,* including the cooked bacon.
- Put the turkey in to roast.

- Marinate the snapper for the *tiradito* skewers.
- Stuff the zucchini cups and refrigerate.

About 2 hours before the buffet:
- Put the *tiradito* skewers together.

Just before guests arrive:
- Make the mulled wine and keep it warm.

15 minutes before the turkey comes out of the oven:
- Start the yuca cooking.

While the turkey is resting:
- Put the stuffing in the oven to heat; wait 15 minutes, then add the zucchini.

While the turkey is being carved:
- Cook the sprouts.
- Finish the *mofongo.*

CHAPTER THREE

Thanksgiving Weekend Brunch

Serves 6

Guava-linis

Baby Spinach Salad with Melon, Almonds,
and Serrano Ham

Crab-*Maduro* Hash with "Eggs, Interrupted" and
Lime Hollandaise

Pumpkin-Spice *Mantecadas*

Many of us are lucky enough to have out-of-town guests for the extended Thanksgiving weekend. If you find yourself hosting friends or family, you'll want to keep the celebration going without wearing yourself out!

Ease into the long weekend with an elegant brunch that won't take hours to prepare. The way I look at it, a house full of people means at least a few pairs of willing hands to help get the menu together. You can also roll some of the do-ahead prep for this menu—such as cleaning the salad greens, measuring out dry and wet ingredients for the muffins, and pre-poaching the eggs—right into your Thanksgiving prep chores.

On the morning of our brunch, I ask my son Erik to man the bar and kick off the festivities with a bubbly, fruity "Daisyfied" take on the Bellini, made with pale pink guava puree. While people are sipping and chatting, my daughter, Angie, mixes up the muffins and I get the hash and hollandaise together in no time. Just after Angie pops those spice-scented muffins into the oven, I sprinkle a couple of teaspoons of vanilla extract onto the coffee grounds and start the pot brewing. When I serve the piping hot coffee, I pour a teaspoon or two of dark rum into each cup to wrap up a lovely, leisurely holiday brunch.

Baby Spinach Salad with Melon, Almonds, and Serrano Ham

MAKES 6 SERVINGS

¼ large (about 6 pounds) honeydew

¼ small (about 5 pounds) seedless watermelon

6 slices country bread or not-too-large *boule*

¼ cup extra-virgin olive oil, plus more for brushing the bread

One 5-ounce bag baby spinach (about 6 cups), washed and dried (preferably in a salad spinner)

Kosher or fine sea salt and freshly ground pepper

2 tablespoons freshly squeezed lime juice

¼ cup Marcona almonds, toasted (see Note)

12 very thin slices serrano ham or prosciutto

1. Scrape out any seeds from the honeydew. (Don't worry about removing the few tiny seeds you will find in the watermelon.) Using the small end of a melon baller, cut both melons into balls. You will need 3 to 4 cups for the salad. Alternatively, cut the melons into ½-inch dice. Save the rest of the melons for another use. The melon balls can be prepared up to the day before serving and refrigerated.

2. Preheat the oven to 375°F. Lightly brush both sides of the bread slices with olive oil and put them on a baking sheet. Bake until lightly browned and crisp, about 15 minutes. Turn once during the baking.

3. To serve: Center 1 slice of toast on each of 6 serving plates. Toss the spinach with the ¼ cup olive oil. Season the spinach with salt (go lightly—the ham will add more salt) and pepper. Add the melon balls, sprinkle the lime juice over the greens, and toss until the greens and melon are coated with dressing. Mound some of the salad over each slice of toast and sprinkle the almonds over the salad. Crisscross 2 slices of ham over the salad and serve immediately.

NOTE: To toast the almonds, spread them out on a baking sheet and bake in a 350°F oven, stirring once or twice so they cook evenly, until golden brown, about 15 minutes.

Baby Spinach Salad with Melon, Almonds, and Serrano Ham and Guava-linis.

Crab-*Maduro* Hash with "Eggs, Interrupted" and Lime Hollandaise

MAKES 6 SERVINGS

There are all kinds of hash in the world—crispy panfried hash, hash enriched with cream for a rich finish, and baked hash, to name a few. This hash is loosely textured and mildly sweet from the addition of *maduros* (sweet ripe plantains). Its crumbly texture makes a perfect bed for 2 runny poached eggs. The hollandaise can be made and kept warm before you even start the hash, and the eggs can be partially poached up to a day in advance. Interrupt the poaching by plunging them into a bowl of ice water and pick up where you left off the next morning while the hash is kept warm in the oven. With these simple do-aheads, you'll be able to pull this whole plate together in no time flat.

FOR THE "EGGS, INTERRUPTED":
1 tablespoon white or cider vinegar
12 jumbo eggs

———————

Lime Hollandaise (page 47)

FOR THE HASH:
¼ cup olive oil
1 large yellow onion, cut into ½-inch dice
(about 2 cups)
1 medium yellow bell pepper, cored,
seeded, and cut into ½-inch dice
(about 1 cup)

1 medium red bell pepper, cored, seeded,
and cut into ½-inch dice (about 1 cup)
1 ripe (mostly black skin but speckled with
yellow) medium plantain, peeled and
cut into ¼-inch dice (2 generous cups)
Kosher or fine sea salt and freshly ground
pepper
Finely grated zest of 1 lime
1 pound lump crabmeat, picked over for
shell and cartilage
2 tablespoons chopped fresh cilantro
(include all but the thickest stems)

Make the "Eggs, Interrupted" and the hollandaise:

1. Pour enough cold water into a large, deep nonreactive skillet to fill to 1 inch from the top. Add the vinegar and heat to simmering. Set a medium bowl of ice water near the pan.

Carefully break one egg at a time into the skillet, making sure not to break the yolk. (If you like, you can break the eggs into a shallow saucer one at a time and slide them into the liquid.) Add as many eggs to the skillet as will fit comfortably. *(Add them going in a clockwise direction, so you know which ones went in first and which should come out first.)* Poach until the whites are barely set but the yolks are still very runny, 3 to 4 minutes. Remove the eggs very carefully with a slotted spoon and slip them into the bowl of ice water. Repeat as necessary with the remaining eggs.

2. Let the eggs stand in the ice water until completely chilled, about 20 minutes. Remove to a clean bowl of cold water and store in the refrigerator up to 24 hours.

3. Make the hollandaise and keep warm (for up to 30 minutes).

Make the hash:

4. Preheat the oven to 200°F.

5. Heat 3 tablespoons of the olive oil in a large, deep ovenproof skillet over medium-high heat. Add the onion and bell peppers and cook, stirring, until the onion is translucent, about 4 minutes. Add the plantain, season lightly with salt and pepper, and lower the heat to medium. Cook and stir until the plantain is softened and glossy and looks a little like cooked pumpkin, 4 to 5 minutes. Stir in the lime zest and the remaining 1 tablespoon olive oil. Remove the pan from the heat and stir in the crabmeat and cilantro. Stir very gently to avoid breaking up the lumps of crab. Pop the whole skillet into the oven to keep the hash warm while rewarming (or poaching) the eggs.

6. To serve, fill a deep skillet halfway with salted water and bring to a simmer over low heat. Slip the "Eggs, Interrupted" into the skillet and heat until the eggs are heated through but the yolks are still runny, about 2 minutes. Scoop about 1 cup of the hash onto the center of a warm plate. One at a time, remove 2 of the eggs from the water with a slotted spoon, draining well before serving. *(To drain the eggs as thoroughly as possible, hold each in the slotted spoon over the water for a few seconds, then blot the bottom of the slotted spoon with a kitchen towel or wad of paper towels.)* Set the 2 eggs over the serving of hash and nap the eggs with about ¼ cup of the sauce. Repeat with the remaining hash, eggs, and sauce, slipping more eggs into the simmering water to rewarm.

NOTE: The eggs can be poached start to finish while the hash is kept warm in the oven if that's your preference. Just add a minute or two to the cooking time for the eggs if starting with raw eggs and serving them right from the skillet.

Lime Hollandaise

MAKES ABOUT 1½ CUPS

Trends come and go, but poached eggs set atop a bed of anything from English muffins to simple crab hash (see page 44) and sauced with hollandaise aren't going anywhere. This is a very straightforward hollandaise except that I've substituted lime juice for the standard lemon juice. Finely grated lime zest adds even more sparkle.

2 extra-large egg yolks
Pinch of cayenne pepper or other pure
    chile powder, or a dash of hot red
    pepper sauce

1 cup warm clarified butter (see Note)
Juice of 1 lime, or to taste
Finely grated zest of 1 lime
Kosher or fine sea salt

1. Pour 2 inches of water into the bottom of a double boiler and bring to a simmer. If you don't have a double boiler, pour 2 inches of water into a wide saucepan and bring to a simmer. Choose a heatproof bowl that sits on top of the saucepan comfortably without the bottom of the bowl touching the water.

2. Whisk the egg yolks, cayenne, and 1 tablespoon water together in the top of the double boiler just until blended. Set over the simmering water and continue whisking until the yolks turn pale yellow and foamy-light and are thickened enough that you can see the bottom of the double boiler as you whisk. Don't be tempted to cheat on the whisking during this stage, or the eggs won't be ready to absorb the butter and you will end up with a heavy sauce.

3. Continue whisking while dribbling in the butter literally a drop at a time until about half the butter has been added. Still whisking, trickle in the remaining butter slowly. If the butter is added too fast or if you slack off on the whisking, the sauce will break.

4. When all the butter has been added, whisk in the lime juice and zest and salt to taste. Serve right away or cover the sauce with a clean kitchen towel and keep warm on a corner of the stove (or other warm place) for up to 30 minutes. An insulated coffee carafe is also a good way to keep the sauce warm.

NOTE: Clarifying butter, that is, removing the milk solids from the butter, is a simple process. Put a little more butter than you need for the recipe in a microwavable container large enough to hold the butter after melting it. (For the above hollandaise recipe, start with 1¼ cups un-salted butter—10 ounces, or 2½ sticks.) Cover the container and microwave at medium power until the butter is completely melted. Let stand until all the milky white solids settle to the bottom. Then simply skim off the foam (if there is any) from the surface and pour the clear yellow butter into a fresh container, leaving the milk solids behind. In addition to this hollandaise, use clarified butter for frying eggs, cooking pancakes, or any recipe where the flavor of butter is welcome but higher heat is needed. Without the milk solids, butter can withstand a much higher heat before it begins to smoke.

Pumpkin-Spice *Mantecadas*

MAKES 12 MUFFINS

As a killer (and simple) spread for these muffins, known as *mantecadas* in Spain, beat a little honey into some softened butter. Serve the honey-butter at room temperature, so it gets into the nooks of the muffins.

Vegetable oil cooking spray

2 cups all-purpose flour

½ cup coarsely chopped pecans

¼ cup granulated sugar

¼ cup packed light brown sugar

1 tablespoon baking powder

1 teaspoon ground cinnamon

½ teaspoon ground nutmeg

½ teaspoon ground cloves

½ teaspoon salt

1 cup canned pumpkin puree (not pumpkin pie filling)

8 tablespoons (1 stick) unsalted butter, melted

2 extra-large eggs

1. Preheat the oven to 350°F. Line a 12-cup muffin tin with paper liners and spray the liners with vegetable oil cooking spray.
2. Stir the flour, pecans, granulated and brown sugars, baking powder, cinnamon, nutmeg, cloves, and salt together in a mixing bowl. In a separate bowl, beat the pumpkin puree, melted butter, and eggs together until well blended. Pour the liquid ingredients into the dry ingredients and fold together with a rubber spatula just until the dry ingredients are evenly moistened. Don't overmix.
3. Divide the batter among the cups, filling each cup almost all the way. Bake until the muffins spring back when poked gently and the edges are browned, about 25 minutes. Serve warm or at room temperature. The muffins can be stored, tightly covered, for up to 2 days. Rewarm them in a low oven or split and toast them before serving.

Guava-linis

MAKES 6 DRINKS

My girlfriend Violette loves to entertain, but she hates to cook; luckily, she has a friend (*moi!*) who loves to do both. Recently, when Vi decided to have a few friends over for brunch, I decided to take the stress out of the event for her and prepare the food. Violette left the menu completely up to me, with one request: The one thing she insisted on was a Bellini (sparkling wine—usually prosecco—and a dash of white peach puree). I decided to swap out the white peach puree for my favorite guava beverage base, and an instant favorite was created!

One 750-milliliter bottle medium-dry white sparkling wine, well chilled
1½ cups Perfect Purée guava beverage base (see Note, page 140)

Juice of 1 lime
Raspberries or sliced strawberries (with or without leaves attached), for garnish

1. Tilting a pitcher on its side, pour 2 cups (a little more than half the bottle) of the sparkling wine into the pitcher. Add the guava puree and lime juice and give it a quick stir.
2. Tilt the pitcher again, and add the rest of the champagne. Pour into flutes and garnish each with a couple of raspberries or a slice of strawberry.

Preparation Schedule

The day or evening before the brunch:
- Prep the salad ingredients:
  - Wash and dry the spinach.
  - Cut the melon balls.
  - Toast the almonds.
- Poach the eggs.
- Measure out the dry ingredients for the *mantecadas*.
- Prep the hash ingredients.

About 30 minutes before brunch:
- Bake the toasts for the salad.
- Make the hollandaise and keep it warm.
- Bring water to a simmer for reheating the eggs.
- Make the muffins and pop them into the oven.

After clearing the salad plates:
- Make the hash and keep it warm in the oven while reheating the eggs.

CHAPTER FOUR

Cocktail Party for a Festive Season

Serves 20

Crispy Potato-Cabrales Wontons

Tuna *Picadillo* in Crisp Cucumber Cups

Mushroom Croquettes

Chipotle-Pork Meatballs (page 146)

Caribbean Spring Rolls

Empanaditas with *Huitlacoche*, Spinach, and Mushroom Filling

Frita Sliders

Sandwichitos (page 66)

Pisco Sours

Mini-Morsel Mexican Wedding Cookies

I always say that no one loves a party more than a Puerto Rican! Whatever the occasion, we start the celebration the day before and look for any excuse to carry it over to the day after. That being said, the winter holiday season is always chock-full of parties in my family. Between Jerry's professional parties, which we host at home, my "foodie" parties, and a slew of family celebrations, there is not always time to arrange a full-blown sit-down dinner party. This is where the cocktail party fits in perfectly.

The pace of a cocktail party seems faster than a leisurely sit-down dinner or even a buffet. To prepare, I always make sure that most of the nibbles are made beforehand, when I've had some time to kill in the kitchen. If quickly frozen and tucked away in freezer-safe plastic bags, my Crispy Potato-Cabrales Wontons, smoky Chipotle-Pork Meatballs, hot and sweet Caribbean Spring Rolls, and *Frita* Sliders can all be made well ahead of time. Last-minute touches, like the crispy-crunchy fried matchstick potatoes that top the *fritas* and the simple soy-ginger sauce for sprinkling over the spring rolls, are finished up hours before the festivities get under way. Even with most of the work done in advance, this is quite a full menu. Feel free to pick and choose, but make sure your menu is balanced, that is, with something for the vegetarian, the seafood lover, *and* the carnivore on your guest list.

As always, enlist willing guests to lend a hand passing trays of food or pouring wine. People love to help; let them! My own trusted crew (husband Jerry and kids!) loves to be part of the action. Angela and David step out of the kitchen with platters full of wontons, *picadillo* in cucumber cups, or whatever else is on the menu and never seem to make it past the dining room. (They know by now to occasionally sneak out the other door of the kitchen, so guests in the living room don't miss out!) If Erik is not available to man the bar, I'll beg Marc to handle the libations, and slip him this recipe for Chilean pisco sours, compliments of my friend Carolina's mom. *Gracias*, Vicky!

'Tis the season for giving, so a parting gift of homemade Mexican wedding cookies, all tied up in cellophane and finished with a pretty ribbon, or even a cheerfully wrapped bottle of your favorite vinegar makes a wonderful party favor for your celebration! It also gives your guests something to remind them of you after the party is over—if the cookies survive the ride home, that is!

Crispy Potato-Cabrales Wontons

**MAKES 64 WONTONS (USING ABOUT 2 CUPS FILLING,
WHICH COULD DOUBLE AS A SIDE DISH FOR 2 OR 3 PEOPLE)**

Think of these as Chino-Latino mini knishes: rich potato filling spiked with Cabrales blue cheese and wrapped in crackling-crisp wonton wrappers. They are delicious on their own or floated in compatible soups, like the Velvety Cauliflower-Pear Soup on page 12.

1 large Idaho or Yukon gold potato (about
    14 ounces), peeled and cut into
    quarters
Kosher or fine sea salt
3 tablespoons unsalted butter
½ cup finely diced onion
¼ cup evaporated milk or evaporated skim
    milk

Freshly ground pepper
¼ cup crumbled Cabrales or other blue-
    veined cheese
75 wonton wrappers (about 4 by 4 inches;
    includes several "security" wrappers)
Vegetable oil, for frying

Make the wontons:

1. Put the potato in a small saucepan, add cold water to cover, and add a heaping teaspoon of salt. Bring to a boil and cook until the potato is tender but not mushy, about 15 minutes.

2. Meanwhile, heat 1 tablespoon of the butter in a small skillet over medium heat. Add the onion, season lightly with salt, and cook, stirring, until golden brown, about 6 minutes. Set aside.

3. Drain the potato and put it in a small bowl. Slice the remaining 2 tablespoons butter and add it to the bowl along with the evaporated milk. Whisk until only a few small lumps remain. Fold in the onion and salt and pepper to taste. Let cool to room temperature, then fold in the Cabrales. Use the filling right away; refrigerating will make it hard and difficult to work with.

4. Place a rounded teaspoonful of potato filling in the center of a wonton wrapper. Moisten the edges of the wrapper with a fingertip dipped in water. Fold two opposite corners to meet over the filling to make a triangle with one long side. Pinch around the edges to seal.

Bring the two corners of the long side together, moisten one of the corners, and pinch them together to form a wonton that looks like a bishop's miter. Repeat with the remaining wrappers. The wontons may be refrigerated for up to several hours or frozen for up to 1 month before cooking. In either case, line up the finished wontons on a baking sheet lined with parchment or waxed paper. Cover refrigerated wontons lightly with a clean kitchen towel. If freezing, put the wontons in the freezer, uncovered, on the baking sheet. When solid to the touch, carefully transfer them to a resealable freezer bag. Remove them to the refrigerator 30 minutes to 1 hour before frying.

Fry the wontons:

5. Pour 2 inches of oil into a large, deep skillet and heat over medium heat until the tip of the handle of a wooden spoon gives off a lively sizzle when immersed in the oil (about 375°F). Carefully slip as many wontons into the oil as will fit without bumping into each other. Fry, turning once, until blistered and golden brown, 3 to 4 minutes. Drain on a baking sheet lined with paper towels. Repeat with the remaining wontons, letting the oil reheat between batches if necessary. Serve warm or hot.

Tuna *Picadillo* in Crisp Cucumber Cups

MAKES ABOUT 24 CUCUMBER CUPS

This dish is all about the tuna. The tuna is served raw, so you need the best, freshest tuna you can get. Buy it on the day you intend to use it and refrigerate it immediately.

3 English (hothouse) cucumbers

½ just-ripe Hass avocado, pitted, peeled, and cut into ¼-inch cubes

1 ripe medium plum tomato, cored, cut in half lengthwise, seeded, and cut into ¼-inch dice (about ⅓ cup)

¼ cup diced (¼-inch) onion

2 tablespoons olive oil

½ jalapeño, seeds left in for more heat, stemmed and finely chopped (about 1½ tablespoons)

1 tablespoon finely chopped fresh cilantro

Juice of 1 lime

Kosher or fine sea salt and freshly ground pepper

1 pound sushi-quality tuna steak, cut into ¼-inch dice (2 cups)

1. Top and tail the cucumbers and cut them crosswise into 1¼-inch lengths. Use a melon baller or an espresso spoon to hollow out the rounds into cups to hold the finished tuna *picadillo.* Leave about ¼ inch of the cuke flesh attached to the sides and bottom of each cup. The cucumbers can be cut a day in advance—wrap them in lightly dampened paper towels, put them in a resealable plastic bag, and refrigerate.

2. Toss the avocado, tomato, onion, olive oil, jalapeño, cilantro, and lime juice gently (to keep the pieces of avocado intact) until mixed. Season with salt and pepper to taste. The tuna can be cut and the avocado-tomato mix can be prepared up to several hours before serving. Refrigerate both separately, but wait until the last minute to combine the two and fill the cuke cups.

3. Just before serving, line up the cucumber cups on a platter. Season the insides of the cups lightly with salt. Toss the tuna and the avocado-tomato mixture together gently. Mound the filling into the prepared cucumber cups and serve immediately.

Clockwise from bottom left: Tuna *Picadillo* in Crisp Cucumber Cups, Caribbean Spring Rolls, and Chipotle-Pork Meatballs.

DAISY DOES: **DEEP-FRYING**

This menu features a few fried items among the eight or so savory offerings. Two of those items, the shoestring fries for the *fritas* and the Mushroom Croquettes, can be fried in advance. The fries, because they are so thin, will stay crisp for hours; the croquettes reheat beautifully in a hot oven (see the preparation schedule on page 73 for details). Last-minute frying is limited to the Crispy Potato-Cabrales Wontons (and even those will stay crisp for half an hour or so) and the Caribbean Spring Rolls (which *must* be fried at the last minute). If the idea of last-minute frying still doesn't appeal, swap out those items for others: Double-up on *Sandwichitos* (see page 66), perhaps, or introduce a couple of items from other menus in the book, like the Red Snapper *Tiradito* Skewers on page 22 or the Turkey, Bacon, and Avocado Panini (page 80), served hot and cut into cocktail-size pieces.

Having said that, there really isn't all that much to making crisp, delicious, and nongreasy fried foods, and people do love the occasional treat. Here are a few pointers to keep in mind:

- Choose a heavy pot with high sides, like a sturdy Dutch oven. When some foods are added to hot oil, the oil foams and bubbles. The high sides keep the oil from spilling over. Plus, it's easier to attach a clip-on frying thermometer to a high-sided pot than it is to a shallow skillet.

- Choose an oil with a high "smoke point," which is exactly what it sounds like—the temperature at which an oil will start to smoke. Go with canola, grapeseed (warning: pricey!), or peanut oil and avoid olive oil or any flavored oils.

- Set up before you fry: Line a baking sheet with a double thickness of paper towels for draining and set it near the deep-frying pot. Set out a wide skimmer with large holes, aka a "spider." Spiders have more surface area for scooping and bigger holes for draining oil faster than slotted spoons.

- My trusty wooden-spoon method (see pages 60 and 65) works well as a general gauge of oil temperature, but if you want complete accuracy (useful for frying several items, as you're doing with this menu), invest in an inexpensive frying thermometer.

- Finally, add only as many pieces to the oil as will float around freely. Whenever you add room-temperature food to hot oil, the temperature of the oil will drop. One of the keys to successful frying is to keep the oil temperature from dropping too much. After scooping out the food, check the temperature on the thermometer and give the oil a minute or two to reheat if it needs it.

Mushroom Croquettes

MAKES 24 CROQUETTES

1 double recipe Mushroom *Picadillo* (page 13)

2 tablespoons unsalted butter

2½ tablespoons all-purpose flour

¾ cup milk

¼ to ⅓ cup fine dry bread crumbs, plus 1 cup more for coating the croquettes

Kosher or fine sea salt and freshly ground pepper

2 eggs

1 cup panko bread crumbs, or as needed

Canola or vegetable oil, for frying

1. Make the *picadillo*—one batch at a time—and scrape it into a mixing bowl.

2. Make the béchamel: Melt the butter in a small saucepan over medium heat. Whisk in the flour and cook until the roux changes from thick and pasty to light and bubbly. Whisk in the milk. Bring to a boil, whisking constantly. Adjust the heat so the sauce is simmering and cook until smooth and very thick. Whisk the whole time, reaching into the corners of the pan so the sauce doesn't stick and burn. Scrape the béchamel into the bowl with the mushroom *picadillo*, add ¼ cup fine bread crumbs, and stir very well. Season with salt and pepper to taste. Refrigerate for 30 minutes to an hour. If the mixture isn't firm enough to hold together when you roll a little of it into a ball, stir in additional fine bread crumbs. The croquette mixture may be made to this point up to 1 day in advance and refrigerated.

3. Form the croquettes: Working with 2 tablespoons of the mushroom mix for each, make log-shaped croquettes about 1½ inches long. Lay them out on a baking sheet as you work.

4. Coat the croquettes: Beat the eggs together with a few drops of water in a shallow bowl. Spread out 1 cup of fine bread crumbs and the panko bread crumbs on separate plates. Roll a croquette in the fine bread crumbs until coated, then slip it into the eggs. Roll the croquette around until coated and hold it over the bowl for a few seconds to let the excess egg drip back into the bowl. Lay the croquette in the plate of panko and shake the plate to coat the croquette with crumbs on all sides. Pat the bread crumbs onto the croquette to help them stick. Shake off the excess crumbs. Repeat with the remaining croquettes,

lining them up on a clean baking sheet as you go. The croquettes may be shaped and breaded up to several hours before frying. Refrigerate them on their baking sheet lightly covered with plastic wrap.

5. Fry the croquettes: Heat 2 inches of oil in a heavy pot over medium heat until the tip of the handle of a wooden spoon dipped in the oil gives off a steady sizzle (about 350°F). Slip as many croquettes into the oil as will fit without crowding and cook, turning them as necessary, until a deep golden brown on all sides and heated through, about 3 minutes. Adjust the heat under the pot during cooking to keep the oil as close to 350°F as possible. Remove and drain the croquettes on paper towel–lined plates. Repeat with the remaining croquettes. Serve hot.

Caribbean Spring Rolls

(SEE PHOTO, PAGE 56)

MAKES 24 ROLLS (USING ABOUT 8 CUPS FILLING)

A friend brought the most delicious chorizo-shrimp-plantain "burgers" to a potluck fund-raiser dinner I hosted for Share Our Strength. I loved them and thought that, with a little crunch from Napa cabbage, the trio would make a terrific spring roll filling. Happy to say, I was right. Except for the frying, these spring rolls are made completely ahead of time. At some point during the party, slip into the kitchen and fry off a bunch of these—it takes only a few minutes—and pass them around while good and hot.

FOR THE FILLING:

2 tablespoons olive oil

1 medium yellow onion, cut into ½-inch dice (about 1¾ cups)

2 links hot or sweet Spanish chorizo (about 7 ounces), cut into ¼-inch dice (about 1½ cups)

1 pound small shrimp (about 40 per pound), peeled, deveined, and cut crosswise into 4 pieces each (about 2 cups)

Kosher or fine sea salt and freshly ground pepper

2 mostly ripe (more or less equal parts
yellow and black skin) medium
plantains, peeled and cut into ¼-inch
dice (2 generous cups)

½ small (about 1 pound) Napa cabbage,
cored and finely chopped (about
4 cups)

½ cup chopped fresh cilantro (include all
but the thickest stems)

Juice of 1 lime

24 spring roll wrappers (about
7 by 7 inches)

1 egg, well beaten

**FOR THE SPRINKLING SAUCE
AND FRYING:**

¼ cup soy sauce

¼ teaspoon grated fresh ginger

Vegetable oil, for frying

Make the filling:

1. Heat the olive oil in a large skillet over medium-high heat. Add the onion and cook, stirring, just until it turns translucent, about 4 minutes. Add the chorizo and cook, stirring, until the chorizo is shiny and fragrant, about 3 minutes. Stir in the shrimp, and season lightly with salt (careful with the salt because of the chorizo) and pepper. Stir and cook for a minute or two. Gently stir in the plantains and cook, shaking the pan, until the shrimp are cooked through, about 2 minutes. Remove from the heat and let cool.

2. When cool, stir in the Napa cabbage, cilantro, and lime juice. Season with salt and pepper to taste.

Make the spring rolls:

3. Place a spring roll wrapper on the countertop with one of the corners pointing toward you. Brush the far corner of the wrapper with the beaten egg. Scoop ⅓ cup of the filling onto the center of the spring roll wrapper and spread it out to make a 1-inch-wide rectangular strip that covers the center of the wrapper and runs from right to left, leaving a 1-inch border on either side. Fold the corner pointing toward you over the filling, pressing it down gently so it hugs the filling. Fold the left and right corners over the filling, making sure no filling is peeking through the ends—tuck and pleat the wrapper as necessary to keep the filling enclosed. Starting at the bottom, roll the spring roll up into a snug but not-too-tight bundle. Make sure the egged edges are sealed and no filling is visible. If you can see any gaps, that means oil will seep into the filling during frying—not a pretty picture. Repeat with the remaining wrappers. The spring rolls can be made up to a few weeks in

Brush the far corner of the spring roll wrapper with beaten egg.

Mound the filling in the center of the wrapper, keeping it about 1 inch from the edges.

After folding the lower corner of the wrapper over the filling, fold in both side corners so the filling is completely encased.

advance and frozen. Line them up on a parchment- or waxed paper–lined baking sheet and freeze until solid before transferring them to a resealable freezer bag. Before cooking, spread them out on a baking sheet so they aren't touching and defrost them at room temperature for about 30 minutes before frying.

Make the sauce and fry the spring rolls:

4. Stir the soy sauce and ginger together in a small bowl and set aside. Pour enough oil into a heavy pot to fill about 2 inches. Heat over medium heat until the tip of the handle of a wooden spoon gives off a very lively sizzle (about 390°F). Very carefully, slip as many of the spring rolls into the oil as will fit without bumping into one another. Fry until the undersides are a deep golden brown and blistered, about 2 minutes. Flip the rolls and repeat. Drain on a baking sheet lined with paper towels and fry the next batch.

5. To serve: When all are fried, cut the spring rolls in half on a pronounced diagonal. Arrange the halves, cut side up, on a platter. *(If you have one, choose a wide, shallow serving bowl or platter with a "well" in the center so you can prop up the cut rolls side by side, which will make it easy to sprinkle the sauce over the filling as well as keep the rolls warm and keep the filling from spilling out.)* Give the soy-ginger sauce a good stir and sprinkle it very lightly over the filling. Serve immediately.

Empanaditas with Huitlacoche, Spinach, and Mushroom Filling

MAKES ABOUT 36 COCKTAIL-SIZE OR 16 LARGE EMPANADAS (SEE NOTES)

Huitlacoche, or Mexican truffle, is difficult to find fresh here in the United States. But luckily, it is readily available in cans in many Latin markets and even supermarkets with a decent Latin food aisle. I first tasted *huitlacoche* empanadas while enjoying an alfresco lunch in the zocalo, or big central square, in Oaxaca. The empanada was filled with the inky black *huitlacoche* accompanied by garlic-sautéed *chaya* leaves—a plant that tastes like spinach with a little kick. I was an instant believer!

The earthy, mushroomy flavor and aroma of *huitlacoche* would also make a nice addition to tamales or tacos, or even sauces and soups.

1 pound fresh spinach, thick stems, if any, removed

One 7-ounce can *huitlacoche* (see headnote)

2 to 3 tablespoons olive oil

8 ounces button mushrooms, sliced thin (about 2½ cups)

4 cloves garlic, minced

⅓ cup raisins (optional)

¼ cup coarsely shredded Manchego cheese

Kosher or fine sea salt and freshly ground pepper to taste

Two 10-ounce packages large (6-inch) empanada wrappers (see Notes), defrosted if necessary

1 egg, beaten

Make the filling:

1. Bring a large pot of salted water to a boil. Set a colander in the sink and a large bowl of ice water near the sink. Stir the spinach into the boiling water and cook, stirring constantly, until the spinach is bright green and tender, 1 to 2 minutes. Drain the spinach immediately and set the colander in the bowl of ice water. Drain again, then press as much water out of the spinach as you can with your hands. Chop the spinach coarsely and set aside.

2. Empty the can of *huitlacoche* into a strainer set over a bowl, shaking gently to remove as much liquid as possible.

3. Heat 2 tablespoons olive oil in a large skillet over medium heat. Add the mushrooms and cook, stirring, until most of the liquid given off by the mushrooms has evaporated. Drizzle a bit more oil into the pan if the pan looks dry, and add the garlic. Cook until the mushrooms are softened, 1 to 2 minutes. Stir in the spinach and raisins, if using, and cook, stirring, until any water remaining in the spinach has cooked off. Stir the drained *huitlacoche* gently into the spinach mixture in the pan. Set aside to cool.

4. Once the spinach mixture has cooled, add the shredded cheese and season the filling with salt and pepper to taste.

Form the *empanaditas*:

5. Cut the empanada wrappers in half. Moisten the edges of one of the half-wrappers with a fingertip dipped in warm water. Center 2 tablespoons of the filling on the wrapper. Bring the sides of the wrapper together to meet over the filling and form a wedge shape. Pinch the sides together and seal the edges all the way around by pressing firmly with the tips of the tines of a fork. The *empanaditas* can be filled up to several hours before serving. Refrigerate them on a parchment- or waxed paper–lined baking sheet.

6. About 30 minutes before serving, preheat the oven to 375°F. Line a baking sheet with parchment paper (or use a nonstick baking sheet). Brush the *empanaditas* lightly with the beaten egg and bake until the *empanaditas* are a light golden brown, about 25 minutes. Let cool for a few minutes before serving.

NOTES

- Plain (off-white) or flavored empanada wrappers are available frozen (and sometimes refrigerated) in many supermarkets and almost all Latin markets.
- To make large empanadas, place ¼ cup of filling in the center of each whole wrapper. Moisten the edges of the wrapper and fold into a half-moon shape. Press the edges firmly together all the way around with the tips of the tines of a fork to seal.

Frita Sliders

MAKES TWENTY-FOUR 2½-INCH PATTIES

If you visit *Calle Ocho* (Eighth Street), Miami's Cuban neighborhood, try the *fritas*—Cuban burgers seasoned with achiote and topped with a haystack of shoestring fries.

FOR THE BURGERS:

1 medium yellow onion, cut into large
  chunks
1½ pounds ground pork
1½ pounds ground beef
1 tablespoon kosher or fine sea salt
1 teaspoon freshly ground pepper
2 tablespoons Achiote Oil (page 134), at
  room temperature

FOR THE SHOESTRING FRIES:

Canola or vegetable oil, for frying
1 medium Idaho potato (about 9 ounces),
  peeled and cut into ⅛-inch matchsticks

FOR SERVING:

24 small (about 2½-inch) rolls
Ketchup

Make the burgers:

1. Chop the onion in a food processor using quick on-off pulses and stopping several times to scrape down the sides of the work bowl until the onion is very finely chopped—almost pureed—and liquidy. Crumble the ground pork and beef into a large mixing bowl. Scatter the onion over the meat, season with salt and pepper, and drizzle the achiote oil over everything. Mix with your hands just until the onion is evenly mixed in and the meat is a nice shade of red.

2. Using ¼ cup for each burger, form the meat mixture into 2½-inch patties, lining them up on a waxed or parchment paper–lined baking sheet as you go. The patties can be refrigerated for up to 1 day or frozen for up to a few weeks. In either case, cover the baking sheet well with plastic wrap and then aluminum foil. Defrost frozen burgers overnight in the refrigerator before cooking.

Make the fries:

3. Pour enough of the oil into a heavy pot to fill to 2½ inches. Heat over medium heat until the tip of the handle of a wooden spoon gives off a very lively sizzle when put into the oil (about 390°F).

4. While the oil is heating, line a baking sheet with a double thickness of paper towels. Blot the potato matchsticks dry with paper towels in batches. When the oil reaches the right temperature, add as many matchsticks to the oil as will fit comfortably—it should be easy to stir them around—and fry until a deep golden brown and crisp, 3 to 4 minutes. Remove with a spider or slotted spoon and drain on the lined baking sheet. Repeat with the remaining matchsticks. Adjust the heat to maintain the oil at a constant temperature while frying. The shoestring fries can be held at room temperature for up to 3 hours.

Cook and serve the burgers:

5. The burgers can be panfried, grilled, or broiled: Set 2 large, heavy skillets over medium heat; or preheat a gas grill to high or build a strong charcoal fire; or set a rack about 6 inches from the broiler and preheat the broiler. Whichever method you choose, cook the burgers, turning them only once, until well browned on the outside and no trace of pink remains in the center. An instant-read thermometer inserted into the center of a fully cooked burger will register 150°F.

6. While the burgers are cooking, split the buns and arrange the bottoms on a serving platter with a bowl of ketchup with a spoon in the center. Put a cooked burger on each roll bottom, top with a mini mound of shoestring fries, and top with the tops of the rolls. Serve right away.

SANDWICHITOS

It's funny how certain foods steal the show whenever they make an appearance. At the fanciest reception, it is always the waiter carrying the tray of pigs-in-a-blanket who gets mobbed. Put out a tray of deviled eggs at a barbecue, and count the seconds until they're all gone. *Sandwichitos*—which are exactly what they sound like, "little sandwiches"—are in that category.

While you can make *sandwichitos* out of just about anything, there is one constant: squishy-soft white bread. Figure 4 *sandwichitos* for each 2 slices of bread. Simply lay out half of the bread slices you'll be using, top them with whatever filling you like, and close up the sandwiches. Trim off the crusts and cut the sandwiches corner-to-corner into triangles. Make them hours ahead, arrange them on a platter, cover, and refrigerate them until about an hour before serving.

Try slider buns (see page 65) instead of sliced white bread for a different take on *sandwichitos*. Or turn to leftovers for inspiration: Try making a *sandwichito* filling with finely chopped leftover roast turkey mixed with sun-dried tomato mayonnaise (see pages 28 and 80). Whatever bread or filling you decide on for your *sandwichitos,* just be sure to make enough!

Pisco Sour

MAKES 8 SERIOUS DRINKS

Whenever you visit a restaurant in Peru, someone will plunk a pisco sour down in front of you within minutes of your being seated. That's a routine I can get used to! After all the restaurants we visited in Peru, I thought I had the pisco sour down pat. And then I met my good friend Carolina's mom, La Vicky, who set me on the road to pisco sour enlightenment. La Vicky's Chilean version puts a small amount of egg white right into the pisco-lime mix. It's just enough to add a little *espuma,* or foam, to the top without adding any eggy flavor. The flavor is pure pisco and lime—and that's the way I love it.

Pisco is a strong spirit distilled from grapes in much the same way as brandy or grappa. It is made in both Chile and Peru and the question of who makes the "true" pisco is a matter of great debate in both countries. Chile and Peru have different means of classifying their piscos. To simplify, there are all grades and qualities ranging from almost clear (and relatively tasteless) through pale yellowish to distinctly yellow-greenish. For a truly great pisco sour, don't skimp when it comes to the pisco. Buy the best you can find and/or afford.

2 cups pisco (see headnote)

⅔ cup fresh lime juice, or to taste

2 to 3 tablespoons superfine sugar, or to taste

1 tablespoon egg white

Ice cubes

Make the mix:

1. Stir the pisco, the lime juice, and 2 tablespoons superfine sugar together. Give it a taste. *(La Vicky declares that any adjustments to the flavor should be made by altering the amount of lime juice or sugar—leave the pisco be.)* When the flavor is right for you, stir in the egg white. The mix can be made several hours before serving.

For 2 drinks:

2. Pour a scant ¾ cup of the pisco mix into a blender jar. Add a few ice cubes and blend until the ice is dissolved and the drink is frothy. Pour into 2 chilled champagne flutes or any tall, tapered glasses. Serve immediately.

Mini-Morsel Mexican Wedding Cookies

MAKES ABOUT 60 COOKIES

Never one to say no to too much of a good thing, I decided to take a perfectly good thing—buttery, nutty Mexican wedding cookies—and make them even better with the addition of fragrant cinnamon and teeny chocolate chips. These are just right with a cup of coffee after a meal or as an afternoon pick-me-up.

1¾ cups walnut pieces

2½ cups all-purpose flour

1 cup tapioca starch (see Notes)

1 teaspoon good-quality ground cinnamon (see Notes)

¼ teaspoon salt

12 ounces (3 sticks) unsalted butter, softened

1 cup granulated sugar

2 tablespoons Grade A dark amber maple syrup

1 teaspoon vanilla extract

1 cup mini chocolate chips

2 cups confectioners' sugar

1. Pulse the walnuts in a food processor until the consistency of coarse cornmeal. Do not overprocess, or they will turn oily and clumpy. *(Spread the walnuts out on a baking sheet and put them in the freezer for 5 minutes before processing. Chilling helps make ground walnuts with a soft, fluffy texture.)* Sift together the flour, tapioca starch, cinnamon, and salt. In the bowl of an electric mixer fitted with the paddle attachment (or in a mixing bowl using a handheld electric mixer) on medium speed, beat the butter and granulated sugar together until light in color and fluffy, about 4 minutes. Drizzle in the maple syrup and vanilla and beat until blended. Reduce the mixer speed to low and add the dry ingredients one third at a time, beating just until each addition is blended in. Raise the mixer speed to medium and beat just until the dough is smooth. Add the ground walnuts and the chocolate chips and mix briefly, just until they're distributed evenly through the dough. Roll the dough into a ball, flatten it into a disk, and wrap in plastic wrap. Chill for at least 30 minutes before shaping the cookies. The dough can be refrigerated for up to 1 week.

2. Preheat the oven to 350°F. Line one or more baking sheets with parchment paper. Working with 1 tablespoon of the dough at a time, roll the dough between your palms into a 2-inch log, then shape the dough into a crescent. Line up the crescents about 1 inch apart on the prepared baking sheet(s). Bake just until the bottom edges start to turn golden, about 20 minutes.

3. Let the cookies cool for 10 minutes on the baking sheet(s), then transfer the cookies to a cooling rack and let cool completely, about 20 minutes.

4. Put the confectioners' sugar in a shallow bowl. Dip the cooled cookies one by one in the sugar to coat them completely. Tap off the excess sugar. Pile up the cookies on a serving plate if serving immediately or store them in an airtight container for up to 1 week.

NOTES

- Tapioca starch is available in some supermarkets and health food stores. It is also available online from Bob's Red Mill, where it is called tapioca flour, at www.bobsredmill.com.
- I remember the econo-size cans and jars of spices that lined the shelves of my grandmother's spice cabinet. I go for smaller jars of the best-quality spices I can find. For these cookies, I prefer China Tung Hing cassia cinnamon or Vietnamese extra-fancy cassia cinnamon, both available from Penzeys (www.penzeys.com). Whatever type you choose, make sure your cinnamon is fresh and sweet-smelling before you commit to making these cookies.

VARIATION: Flavor the confectioners' sugar with 2 tablespoons of unsweetened cocoa powder, making sure the two are very well mixed before coating the cooled cookies.

Preparation Schedule

3 to 4 weeks before the party:
- Make and freeze any or all of these (if not freezing, see the individual recipes for info on making ahead and refrigerating):
  - Wontons
  - Mushroom *picadillo* (for the croquettes)
  - Spring rolls
  - *Frita* patties

Up to 1 week before the party:
- Make the cookie dough.

Up to 3 days before the party:
- Make the chipotle meatballs and sauce.
- Bake the wedding cookies.

Up to 1 day before the party:
- Make the *empanadita* filling.
- Prep the *sandwichito* fillings.
- Prep the cucumber cups.
- Prep the croquette mixture.

6 to 8 hours before the party:
- Form and bread the croquettes.
- Fill the *empanaditas*.
- Make the *sandwichitos*.
- Make the pisco sour mix.
- Make sure all frozen items are removed from the freezer and put in the refrigerator.

2 to 3 hours before the party:
- Make the soy-ginger sauce.
- Cook the shoestring fries.
- Prep the avocado-tomato mix and tuna for the cucumber cups (but don't mix them yet!).

30 minutes before guests arrive:
- Toss the tuna and avocado-tomato mix and fill the cucumber cups.
- Reheat the meatballs.
- Bake the *empanaditas*.
- Set up buns on trays for the *fritas*.
- Fry the croquettes.

As guests arrive:
- Shake and serve pisco sours.
- Put out *sandwichitos* and filled cucumber cups.
- Fry the first batch of wontons.

Periodically during the party:
- Refill trays of *sandwichitos* and filled cucumber cups.
- Fry spring rolls and additional wontons.
- Reheat croquettes and *empanaditas*.
- Cook *fritas* and top with fries.

CHAPTER FIVE

Open House Decorating Party

Serves 12

Cola de Mono ("Monkey's Tail" Milk Punch)

Peruvian Beef Noodle Soup

Creamy Chicken-Lime Soup

Velvety Cauliflower-Pear Soup (page 12)

Turkey, Bacon, and Avocado Panini

Venezuelan *Pan de Jamón*

Watercress, Red Pear, *Queso Fresco,* and
Pomegranate Salad (page 129)

"Cherry Cordial" Bread Pudding

Every year since my oldest son, Erik, was five years old, we have taken a road trip to a Christmas tree farm in Connecticut on the first Saturday in December to chop down our family tree. Rain, snow, or shine, we trudge through row after row of pine trees, saws in mitten-clad hands, until we find the perfect tree. The kids each take a turn at the saw until we fell the tree, whereupon we all yell, *"Aaaaammmmbbbeeeerrrrr!"* (Marc's term since he was two!). Jerry and the boys drag the tree to the car. Once it's secured to the roof, it's time for our tailgate party, featuring plenty of hot dogs, hot soup, and hot chocolate and accompanied by Christmas music blaring from the car stereo!

The day after our outing, we fill our house with family and friends to help decorate the tree and the house. The price of admission is an ornament for the tree. I knew early on that as we got deeper into the holiday season, people's calendars would fill up with parties and dinners, so I decided on an open house–style party. It centers on sandwiches and soups served in mugs—both easy enough to handle while hanging ornaments and garlands! No matter when people stop by or how long they stay, they can enjoy anything from a full meal to a little nibble or sip to tide them over until the next party.

Our house-decorating party quickly became an eagerly anticipated tradition at Casa Daisy and the all-soup-and-sandwich menu became a recurring theme. I've included a few of my favorite soup recipes selected from the many I have served over the years. The Peruvian Beef Noodle Soup was a dish my family enjoyed while visiting Cuzco, while the Creamy Chicken-Lime Soup is a Mexican-inspired potage. The Venezuelan *pan de jamón* is a recipe that my new buddy Yrving Torrealba from San Francisco shared with me; he told me that this very version was *always* present on his mom's Christmas table. I think this delicious spiral of bread stuffed with salty deli ham, sweet raisins, and briny olives lends itself beautifully to this menu as an alternative to the traditional sandwich. As a closing note, the "Cherry Cordial" Bread Pudding is cozy, homey but festive, and if there is someone in my circle who doesn't love chocolate, they're keeping it a secret!

Cola de Mono

("MONKEY'S TAIL" MILK PUNCH)

MAKES 6 CUPS (8 TO 10 SERVINGS)

Where the name came from is anybody's guess. Most tales point back to Pedro Montt (nicknamed *El mono Montt,* or "Montt, the monkey"), who served as Chile's president in the early part of the twentieth century. After that, things get more than a little vague. Whatever the history, think of this delicious milk punch as an eggless-nog warmed up with cinnamon, cloves, and allspice and given a little kick with espresso powder. A bigger kick comes from Chilean *aguardiente* (literally "firewater"), a high-proof spirit made in a process similar to that used for Italian grappa. If Chilean *aguardiente* isn't available, rum is a good substitute. *Aguardiente* from other Latin countries is often strongly flavored and those flavors won't necessarily marry well with the other ingredients in this *Cola de Mono.*

4 cinnamon sticks

14 whole cloves

12 whole allspice berries

Finely grated zest of 2 oranges

4 cups milk

¼ cup instant espresso powder

1 tablespoon sugar

1½ cups *aguardiente* (see headnote) or
   light rum

1. Put ½ cup water, the cinnamon sticks, cloves, allspice, and orange zest in a small saucepan. Bring to a boil, then adjust the heat so the liquid is barely simmering. Simmer for 5 minutes. Stir in the milk and let steep over very low heat for 10 minutes. Stir in the espresso powder and the sugar. Strain into a serving pitcher and chill thoroughly.

2. Just before serving, stir in the *aguardiente* or rum. Serve very cold in chilled glasses, with or without ice.

Peruvian Beef Noodle Soup (SEE PHOTO, PAGE 83)

(SOPA CRIOLLA)

MAKES ABOUT 10 CUPS (8 LUNCHTIME SERVINGS)

In Peru, *sopa criolla* ("Creole soup") is what they call beef soup. You will find delicious versions of it everywhere, but my favorite was the one my family had at La Casa de Inka, a charming restaurant that featured a fantastic view of the city of Cuzco in addition to its traditional Peruvian cuisine. My son Marc has the uncanny ability to walk into a restaurant he's never been to and pick out the best thing on the menu. He ordered this soup and it was instantly the family favorite.

The big deal is the broth—fragrant and rich with flavor thanks to aromatics like onion, garlic, and bay leaf. As soon as I tasted it, I knew I had to re-create it. The carrots aren't typical, but I like them, so there they are.

2 pounds beef for stew, cut into more or less ½-inch pieces (don't worry too much about trimming all the fat off—a little bit adds to the flavor)

2 tablespoons vegetable oil, or as needed

1 large Spanish onion (about 12 ounces), diced (about 2 cups)

4 to 5 cloves garlic, minced

2 tablespoons tomato paste

1 teaspoon dried oregano

2 bay leaves

Kosher or fine sea salt and freshly ground pepper

8 cups homemade or store-bought beef broth

4 large carrots, peeled and cut into ¼-inch slices (about 2½ cups)

1 medium zucchini (about 8 ounces), cut in half lengthwise, then crosswise into ¼-inch slices

8 ounces *fideos,* other fine egg noodles, or angel hair pasta

1. Rinse the meat under cold water and pat it dry. Heat the oil in a heavy 5-quart soup pot or Dutch oven over medium heat. Add about one third of the beef. Cook, stirring often, until browned on all sides, about 5 minutes. (If the meat gives off liquid, which it probably will, cook until the liquid has boiled off and the meat begins to brown in the remaining fat.) Repeat with the remaining beef, adding a little more oil if necessary. Transfer each batch of beef to a bowl as it is browned. Adjust the heat as the beef is browning so none of the browned bits that stick to the pan burn.

2. Remove the last batch of beef from the pot and add the onion and garlic. Cook, stirring, until the onion is wilted and picks up the browned bits stuck to the bottom of the pan, about 4 minutes. Return the beef to the pot, add the tomato paste, and cook until the paste coats the meat. Add the oregano and bay leaves and season lightly with salt and pepper. Stir for a minute and then pour in the broth. Cover and bring to a boil. Adjust the heat so the liquid is simmering and cook until the beef is very tender, about 1½ hours.

3. Stir in the carrots and zucchini and cook until the carrots are tender, about 15 minutes. Remove the bay leaves and season the soup with salt and pepper to taste. The soup can be prepared to this point and refrigerated for up to 3 days or frozen for up to 2 months. Return to a gentle boil before continuing.

4. While the vegetables are cooking, bring a large pot of salted water to a boil. Add the noodles and cook, stirring gently occasionally, until they are tender, about 4 minutes. *(If you are not sure whether you will be serving all of this soup [or any other noodle soup] at one seating, prepare the soup and noodles separately. Just before serving, cook the noodles as directed, then drain them and toss them in a bowl with 1 tablespoon of vegetable or olive oil. Put some of the noodles in the bottom of each serving bowl and ladle the soup over them. Any remaining noodles can be refrigerated for the next time the soup is served. Even if the noodles clump together after refrigerating, they can be coaxed apart by sprinkling some warm water over them and tossing them gently.)* Drain and add to the soup. Serve hot.

NOTES

- Traditionally, this is not a very vegetably soup, but I added a fair amount of carrots and zucchini to my version to sneak some of those 5 to 7 servings a day into my family's diet. You can go a step further and add thinly sliced or finely diced odds and ends of vegetables from the refrigerator, either when you first serve the soup or into any leftover soup before serving it a second time.

- This is a soup that freezes beautifully, so it's worth it to make twice as much. Freeze it before adding the noodles.

Creamy Chicken-Lime Soup

(SEE PHOTO, PAGE 83)

**MAKES ABOUT 12 CUPS (8 MAIN-COURSE SERVINGS OR
12 TO 16 SERVINGS AS PART OF A FULL MEAL OR BUFFET)**

The simple trick of simmering chicken thighs for less than an hour produces a very respectable broth and enough shredded chicken meat to make a hearty soup. Because this broth is the base for a soup that will be enriched with carrots, celery, lime, and cream, I left the seasoning for the broth part of the soup pretty basic. If you're looking for a more full-flavored broth, add any or all of the following along with the chicken thighs: half a red bell pepper, several cloves of unpeeled garlic, and half a bushy bunch of cilantro or parsley.

10 bone-in chicken thighs (about 3½ pounds)

1 large yellow onion, root end cut off, skin left on

1 bay leaf

2 tablespoons olive oil

3 large shallots, finely chopped (about ⅔ cup)

7 stalks celery, trimmed and cut on the diagonal into ½-inch slices (about 4 cups)

7 slim carrots, peeled and cut into ¼-inch slices (about 2 cups)

1 chayote

2 cups crumbled *fideos*, other fine egg noodles, or angel hair pasta (see step 4 of Peruvian Beef Noodle Soup, opposite)

1 cup heavy cream

Kosher or fine sea salt and freshly ground pepper

Juice and finely grated zest of 1 lime

1. Put the thighs, whole onion, and bay leaf in a large pot. Pour in 14 cups water. Bring to a boil over high heat. Boil for 5 minutes, skimming all the foam and fat from the surface. Adjust the heat so the broth is simmering and cook until the thighs are tender, about 45 minutes. Strain the broth into a large bowl. Set the chicken thighs aside and let cool. Discard the onion and bay leaf. Rinse out the pot.

2. When the chicken is cool enough to handle, discard the skin and bones. Pick over the meat, get rid of any gristle and fat, and shred the meat coarsely.

3. Heat the oil in the rinsed-out pot over medium heat. Add the shallots and cook until soft-

ened, about 2 minutes. Add the celery and carrots and cook, stirring often, until they start to brown, about 8 minutes. Add the strained broth and the chicken meat to the soup and bring to a boil. Cook until the vegetables are tender, about 15 minutes. The soup can be made to this point up to 3 days in advance and refrigerated. Return to a gentle boil over medium heat before continuing.

4. While the vegetables are simmering (or while the soup is reheating), cut the chayote in half and scoop out the large pit at the center. Cut the chayote into ½-inch dice.

5. When the vegetables are tender, stir in the chayote and cook for 2 minutes. Add the *fideos* and cook, stirring, until tender, about 6 minutes. Reduce the heat to very low and stir in the cream and salt and pepper to taste. Stir in the lime juice and zest. Serve immediately.

Turkey, Bacon, and Avocado Panini
(SEE PHOTO, PAGE 83)

MAKES 4 LARGE OR 16 TO 20 HORS D'OEUVRE–SIZE SANDWICHES

This is my tribute to the mother of all panini—the *cubano*. In this version, the smoked turkey gains richness from the buttery avocado, backup smoke and crispiness from the bacon, and a salty-sweet layer of flavor from the sun-dried tomatoes blended with mayonnaise. This last ingredient is my take on *salsa golf,* traditionally a blend of ketchup and mayonnaise. The name mystified me, until I came to realize that *salsa golf* must have been, at some point, a staple on country club menus in some of the Spanish-speaking world. I know I've seen it on menus in Puerto Rico, the Dominican Republic, and Argentina.

FOR THE *SALSA GOLF* (MAKES ABOUT ⅓ CUP):
¼ cup oil-packed sun-dried tomatoes, drained
¼ cup mayonnaise
Juice of ½ lime
Kosher or fine sea salt

FOR THE SANDWICH:

1 loaf soft Italian bread (about 16 inches)

4 ounces thinly sliced smoked turkey

4 ounces thinly sliced serrano ham

6 slices bacon, cooked to crisp

4 ounces not-too-thinly-sliced Jack cheese

¼ cup chopped pickled jalapeños (optional)

½ ripe Hass avocado, pitted, peeled, and cut into thin slices

Make the *salsa golf:*

1. Put the sun-dried tomatoes, mayonnaise, and lime juice in a mini food processor and blend until the tomatoes are finely chopped. Scrape into a bowl. (Alternatively, the tomatoes can be finely chopped by hand and beaten into the mayonnaise along with the lime juice.) Season with salt—carefully, some sun-dried tomatoes are mighty salty.

Make and press the panini:

2. Preheat a sandwich or panini press. (See Note for information on how to make these without a sandwich press.)

3. Meanwhile, split the bread lengthwise and spread both halves of the loaf with the *salsa golf*. Make an even layer of the sliced turkey and top that with the sliced serrano, bacon, and cheese. Arrange the jalapeños, if using, and avocado slices over the other piece of bread and close up the sandwich. Press firmly to make the sandwich stable enough for pressing.

4. Cut the loaf in half crosswise. Press until the sandwich is warmed through and the bread is crisp, about 5 minutes. Cut each sandwich in half crosswise to make 4 large sandwiches. For hors d'oeuvre–size sandwiches, cut each piece into thin slices or slightly thicker (about 2½-inch slices), then from corner to corner into triangles.

NOTE: If you don't have a sandwich press, try this simple improvisation: Warm a large, heavy skillet or griddle (cast iron for either is ideal) over medium-low heat. Lay as many sandwiches in the skillet or on the griddle as will fit comfortably. Weight them—with another skillet if using a skillet or with a baking sheet topped with 2 medium-size cans if using a griddle. In either case, flip the sandwiches once the undersides are toasted and cook until the centers are warmed through and the bread is crisp on both sides.

Venezuelan *Pan de Jamón*

MAKES ABOUT SIXTEEN 1-INCH SLICES

At a restaurant named Destino in San Francisco I met a young man, Yrving Torrealba, who shared this recipe, his mother's, with me. Yrving told me that Christmas in Venezuela wouldn't be Christmas without *pan de jamón.* I'm starting to feel the same way about Christmas in Brooklyn.

1 pound slab bacon, rind removed, cut into ½-inch cubes (about 2½ cups)

1 pound store-bought pizza dough

All-purpose flour, for dusting

9 very thin slices deli ham, or as needed

½ cup coarsely chopped pitted green olives

½ cup raisins

1 egg, well beaten

1. Preheat the oven to 400°F.
2. Put the bacon in a large skillet, pour in ¼ cup water, and place the pan over high heat. Cook, stirring, until the water has boiled off and the bacon starts to sizzle. Reduce the heat to medium and cook, stirring, until the bacon is browned but not hard and dry, about 8 minutes. Drain off and discard the fat.
3. Roll the pizza dough out on a lightly floured surface to a 15 by 18-inch rectangle with one of the short ends closest to you. Arrange the slices of ham barely overlapping to cover most of the surface of the dough, leaving a 1-inch border along the long sides and a 2-inch border along the short sides. Scatter the olives, raisins, and bacon in an even layer over the ham. Fold the untopped short end of the dough closest to you over the filling, then roll up the dough and filling jelly roll style. Tuck the two ends underneath the roll and pinch closed the seam that runs along the length of the roll. Put the roll on a nonstick or parchment paper–lined baking sheet, seam side down. Brush evenly with the beaten egg.
4. Bake until golden brown and the bottom sounds a little hollow when rapped with a knuckle, about 35 minutes. Serve warm or at room temperature, cut into 1-inch slices. This is best eaten within a few hours of baking.

Clockwise from top right: Venezuelan *Pan de Jamón;* Peruvian Beef Noodle Soup; Creamy Chicken-Lime Soup; Turkey, Bacon, and Avocado Panini; and Velvety Cauliflower-Pear Soup.

"Cherry Cordial" Bread Pudding

MAKES 12 GENEROUS SERVINGS

Bread puddings were always reserved for celebrations—not just in Puerto Rico, but all around the Caribbean. That was certainly the case when I was growing up and watching *Abuela* in the kitchen. (For extra-special occasions, we'd add a whole can of fruit cocktail to the mix!) This very simple recipe features a chocolate custard teamed up with two of chocolate's longtime friends: cinnamon and cherries. It has all the appeal of one of those "cherry cordial" candies (a sweet cherry in a liqueur-flavored syrup encased in dark chocolate). Be sure to give the bread enough soaking time so the chocolaty custard penetrates all the way to the center of the bread cubes. (Break a bread cube open to check.)

1 tablespoon unsalted butter

6 cups heavy cream

12 large eggs

1 cup sugar

2 tablespoons rum

One 11½-ounce bag bittersweet chocolate
    chips

1½ cups semisweet chocolate chips

½ teaspoon ground cinnamon

One 10-inch loaf challah bread, cut (crusts
    and all) into ¾-inch cubes (about
    12 cups; see Notes)

1 cup dried cherries (about 5 ounces)

1. Using the butter, grease an 13 by 9-inch baking dish.
2. Beat 2 cups of the cream with the eggs, sugar, and rum in a large bowl until smooth. Heat the remaining 4 cups cream in a medium saucepan until the edges are bubbling. Remove from the heat, add the bittersweet and semisweet chocolate chips, let stand for 1 minute, then whisk until smooth. Whisk in the cinnamon.
3. Slowly pour the chocolate cream into the cream-egg mixture, whisking continuously until the two are blended. Add the bread, turning gently to coat with the chocolate custard mix. Let stand until the bread has soaked up as much of the custard mixture as it will hold, 30 to 45 minutes, depending on how stale the bread is.
4. While the bread is soaking, preheat the oven to 350°F.
5. Stir the cherries into the custard mix. Pour the pudding mixture into the prepared pan. Bake until the edges are set and the center jiggles a little when you wiggle the pan,

40 to 45 minutes. Let cool for at least 30 minutes before serving warm, or let cool completely and serve at room temperature. The pudding is best eaten before it's been refrigerated.

NOTES

- Day-old bread is best for this. It will be easier to cut into cubes and, as an added bonus, will soak up more chocolaty custard the next day.
- The bread pudding is best eaten warm or at room temperature without ever having seen the inside of a refrigerator. Refrigerated bread pudding just won't have that same creamy-custardy texture, but leftovers will still be quite delicious. If you would like to warm them, do so gently, wrapped in aluminum foil on a baking sheet in a 250°F oven.

Preparation Schedule

3 to 4 weeks before the open house:
- Prepare the chicken and beef soups through step 3 (without the noodles), if freezing.
- Make the cauliflower-pear soup and freeze.

2 to 3 days before the open house:
- Prepare the chicken and beef soups through step 3 (without the noodles), if not freezing.

1 day before the open house:
- Make the *salsa golf* for the panini.
- Prep all the ingredients and the dressing for the salad.
- Cut the bread for the pudding.

Early on the day of the open house:
- Assemble the panini and refrigerate until pressing.
- Make the *Cola de Mono*.

About 4 hours before the open house:
- Make the custard mix for the pudding and soak the bread; when the bread is fully soaked, bake the pudding.
- Cook the bacon for the *pan de jamón*.
- Cook, drain, and refrigerate the noodles for the soups.

About 2 hours before the open house:
- Assemble and bake the *pan de jamón*.

As guests arrive:
- Put out some of the salad and dressing, the *pan de jamón,* and the first round of soups.

Periodically during the open house:
- Replenish hot soups and salad and dressing.
- Press, cut, and serve panini.

As things are wrapping up:
- Serve the bread pudding, warming it up a bit if you feel as though it needs it.

CHAPTER SIX

Christmas Eve Dinner for Your Six Best Friends

Serves 8

Tamarind Margaritas

Ruby Grapefruit Ceviche

Cream of Watercress Soup

Arroz con Pato

Cheese and Fruit

Holidays in my home center on our large family and a host of friends and neighbors both new and old. However, I realize not everyone has the tribe that calls our house their home during the holidays. If you have a smaller family or the lovely tradition of spending Christmas Eve (or any quiet night during the holidays) with near and dear friends, this is a very special menu for those very special guests.

This menu features *the* recipe in this book that requires a bit more effort than the others, *Arroz con Pato* (Luscious Duck with Rice). It is a festive, no-holds-barred dish and the rewards will well justify the extra endeavor. *Arroz con Pato* is to Peruvians what rice with pigeon peas is to Puerto Ricans—that is to say, something of a national obsession. The sweetness of the duck plays nicely off the little bit of heat in the rice, and the pretty verdant rice is a meal in itself. It's small wonder that Jerry always goes back for a second portion!

The extra time that you spend in the kitchen putting together the rice and duck is balanced by the rest of the menu, which is a cinch. I do, however, put some time aside the night before the big event to juice lemons and limes and to get the Ruby Grapefruit Ceviche "cooking" in the refrigerator, ready to make its grand entrance as the perfect start to your dinner. The Cream of Watercress Soup can also be made ahead of time and gently reheated for an elegant first course. My son Erik, who fancies himself the cheese maven, usually brings some fabulous cheeses, which I serve with some lovely pears to close out the meal. What more could you ask for?

Ruby Grapefruit Ceviche

MAKES ABOUT 5 CUPS (ENOUGH FOR 8 FIRST-COURSE SERVINGS OR
16 COCKTAIL SERVINGS)

This is a recipe I came up with after tinkering around with an almost-all-grapefruit ceviche. I found out that the seafood didn't "cook" properly in grapefruit juice, so I turned to a more traditional mix of lemon and lime juice for curing the seafood and a fresh hit of grapefruit juice just before serving. The tart-sweetness of grapefruit, the twang of cilantro, and the fresh mint note make a very nice combination.

1 pound small shrimp (about 40 per
    pound), peeled and deveined
1 pound bay scallops
10 lemons (give or take)
10 limes (give or take)
Kosher or fine sea salt

2 ruby grapefruits or 4 blood oranges
3 tablespoons chopped fresh cilantro
2 tablespoons olive oil
1½ tablespoons chopped fresh mint
Good-quality corn chips, popcorn, or corn
    nuts (optional), for serving

1. Cut the shrimp crosswise into pieces about the same size as the scallops. Put the shrimp and scallops in a tall, narrow container that holds them snugly. *(Using a tall, narrow container means you'll need to squeeze fewer limes and lemons to get enough juice to completely cover the seafood.)* Squeeze as many lemons and limes (roughly the same amount of each) as necessary to cover the seafood with juice (approximately 3 cups). Pour the juice over the seafood, season lightly with salt, and swish the liquid around to dissolve the salt. Cover the container. Refrigerate until the seafood is "cooked" all the way through, 12 to 24 hours. (Cut or bite into a piece; it should be opaque all the way through.)

2. Drain the seafood and transfer it to a serving bowl. With a paring knife, cut away the peel and pith from the grapefruits. Working over the bowl of seafood, cut the segments free from the membrane. Squeeze the juice from the membranes over the seafood. Add the cilantro, olive oil, and mint and toss very gently. If serving as a first course, spoon the ceviche into chilled coupe or martini glasses. Poke a couple of corn chips into the ceviche and pass more around the table separately.

Arroz con Pato

(LUSCIOUS DUCK WITH RICE)

MAKES 8 SERVINGS

This is probably the most technically challenging recipe in the book—unless you can coerce your butcher to cut up and bone the ducks. Putting the dish together after that isn't very hard, but it does take some time, which can be spread out over 2 days. The *sofrito* that gets the rice going is made with onion, chiles, garlic, and cilantro and is like my lifeline *sofrito* on page 134, minus the tomatoes and red bell pepper. That and the spinach lend the rice a beautiful shade of green. The recipe makes more *sofrito* than you will need for this dish: Freeze any extra and add it to your next bean soup or braised chicken dish. If you're not into that idea, simply cut the *sofrito* ingredients in half and you will have the amount of *sofrito* you need for this recipe.

FOR THE DUCKS AND BROTH:

2 whole ducks, preferably fresh, but
  defrosted if frozen (about 5 pounds
  each)

Kosher or fine sea salt and freshly ground
  pepper

4 medium carrots, peeled and cut in half
  crosswise

4 stalks celery, trimmed and cut in half
  crosswise

2 large yellow onions, cut into 2-inch
  chunks

2 serrano chiles or chiles of your choice

2 bay leaves

1 teaspoon whole black peppercorns

FOR THE RICE:

1 very large yellow onion, cut into 2-inch
  chunks

1 bunch fresh cilantro

2 serrano chiles

6 cloves garlic, peeled

2 tablespoons olive oil

4 teaspoons kosher or fine sea salt

4 cups long-grain rice

One 10-ounce box frozen spinach,
  defrosted and as much excess liquid
  squeezed out as possible

Prepare the ducks:

1. For each duck, remove any giblets and the neck from the body cavity. Set the livers aside for another use and put the neck and any remaining giblets in a bowl. Remove the boneless breast halves from the duck: Feel the keel bone that runs down the center of the breast. With a boning or thin-bladed knife, make a cut along one side of the keel bone down to the breastbone. Working mostly with the tip of the knife, feel your way along the curve of the breastbone, separating the meat from the bone as you go. Cut the breast meat away from the wing joint when you get to that point. Cut through the fat near the backbone to free the boneless breast half in one piece. Repeat with the other breast half.

2. Bend one of the legs outward and away from the backbone so you can see the joint that attaches the leg to the backbone. Again working with the tip of the knife, carefully separate the leg at the joint. Once you've cut through the joint, cut the leg completely away from the body. Repeat with the other leg. Trim any excess skin and fat from the legs, breasts, and body of the duck. (There should be just enough fat on the breasts and legs to cover the meat.)

Recap: You should now have 4 trimmed boneless duck breast halves, 4 trimmed legs, and the bodies of 2 ducks with the wings attached, plus the necks and giblets. Blot the breast and legs dry with paper towels and season all sides of them generously with salt and pepper. Refrigerate the seasoned breasts until needed.

Cook the duck legs, make the broth, and make the _sofrito_:

3. Preheat the oven to 400°F.

4. Rinse the duck bodies, necks, and giblets thoroughly under cold water. Blot them dry with paper towels and put them in a roasting pan. Scatter the carrots, celery, onions, and serranos around them. Put a rack in a separate smaller roasting pan and put the legs, skin side up, on the rack. Roast until the duck bodies are mahogany brown, about 1 hour, and the legs are cooked through (no trace of pink near the knee joint), about 1 hour and 15 minutes.

5. As soon as they are done, put the duck bodies, necks, giblets, and vegetables (not the duck legs) into a large pot. Add the bay leaves, peppercorns, and 14 cups water. Bring to a boil over high heat, then adjust the heat so the liquid is simmering. Cook, skimming any foam and fat that rises to the surface, for 1½ hours. Strain the broth and discard the solids. Let

the broth cool to room temperature, then refrigerate until chilled (see Notes). The broth may be made up to 2 days in advance.

6. As soon as the duck legs are cooked, remove them from the oven and let them cool to room temperature.

7. While the broth is simmering and the duck legs are cooling, make the *sofrito:* Process the onion, cilantro, serranos, and garlic in a food processor until very finely chopped. The *sofrito* may be made up to 2 days in advance. You will need 1 cup of *sofrito* to start the rice—refrigerate that amount and freeze or refrigerate any leftover *sofrito* separately for another use (see headnote).

8. When the legs are cool enough to handle, remove the skin in as large pieces as possible. Scrape any excess fat from the underside of the skin. Cut the skin into ¼-inch strips and refrigerate until needed. Pull the leg meat from the bones, shredding it coarsely and removing any fat and gristle as you go. The duck legs may be cooked and shredded up to 2 days in advance.

Recap: You now have all the components needed to make the *arroz con pato:* duck broth, shredded cooked duck leg meat, crispy duck skin for garnish, and seasoned boneless breasts.

Make the rice:

9. Heat the olive oil in a heavy 3- to 4-quart pot or Dutch oven. Add 1 cup of the *sofrito* and cook until the liquid has evaporated and the *sofrito* starts to sizzle. Add the salt, then stir in the rice and cook, stirring, until the rice turns chalky, 3 to 4 minutes. Add the shredded duck leg meat and pour in enough duck broth to cover the rice by 1 inch. Bring to a boil and cook until the level of the broth meets the top of the rice. Scatter the spinach over the top of the rice, give the rice a great big stir, and cover the pot. Cook, without lifting the lid or stirring, until the rice is tender with a little bit of bite and all the broth has been absorbed, 20 minutes.

10. As soon as you add the duck broth to the rice, start cooking the duck breasts. Put them, skin side down, in a cold heavy pan (cast iron is ideal). Put them over low heat and cook until much of the fat is rendered from the skin and the skin is crisp and golden brown, about 15 minutes. Pour off all the fat from the pan and increase the heat to medium. Flip the duck breasts and cook until medium-rare (or however you like them). Transfer them to a plate and keep them in a warm place until the rice is done.

11. Add the reserved duck skin to the pan and cook over medium-low heat until the skin starts to sizzle. Drain on paper towels.

To serve:

12. Cut the duck breasts on the diagonal into ¼- to ½-inch slices. Spoon some of the rice onto each serving plate and fan several slices of the duck breast out over the rice. Scatter some of the crisped-up skin over all.

> **NOTES:**
> - Any fat that wasn't removed from the duck broth will be easy to remove once the broth has chilled. The fat will rise to the top and solidify.
> - This makes more duck broth than you will need for this recipe. Leftover broth may be refrigerated for up to 1 week or frozen for up to 3 months. It would be a lovely replacement for the water in any mushroom and/or vegetable soup, or, if you've decided to use the leftover *sofrito* to kick a pot of white rice into high gear, you could replace some of the water with duck broth and really go for it!

Cream of Watercress Soup

MAKES 8 SERVINGS (ABOUT 9 CUPS)

Cream soups can be whipped up in a flash with any number of ingredients. Cress is a perfect example: It cooks in minutes and lends a peppery, herby zip to a velvety smooth soup that's delicious hot or cold. I gained new respect for watercress after our family's trip to Spain, where it is used in so many innovative ways from soups to salads and even as a side dish, steamed and served very simply with a lemon and olive oil dressing.

8 cups homemade or store-bought
   chicken broth
3 bunches watercress, trimmed of stem
   ends and wilted or yellow leaves
   (about 8 cups)
4 tablespoons (½ stick) unsalted butter

¼ cup minced shallots
¼ cup all-purpose flour
1 tablespoon bottled horseradish
1 cup heavy cream
Kosher or fine sea salt and freshly ground
   pepper

1. Bring the chicken broth to a boil in a medium saucepan over medium-high heat. Meanwhile, wash the cress in cool water, then dry well, preferably in a salad spinner. Stir in the watercress and return to a boil. Strain the broth into a large measuring cup or heatproof bowl. Pulse the watercress in the work bowl of a food processor until finely chopped. With the motor running, add as much of the broth as necessary to make a smooth puree.

2. Wipe out the saucepan. Add the butter and heat over medium heat until foaming. Add the shallots and cook until softened and fragrant, about 2 minutes. Whisk the flour into the shallot mixture and cook until the roux is smooth and bubbling but not at all browned, about 3 minutes. Pour the remaining chicken broth into the pan, whisking all the time to mix thoroughly, then add the pureed watercress. Add the horseradish and stir in the cream. Heat to simmering and season with salt and pepper to taste. Serve right away in warm bowls or let cool to room temperature, then chill. The soup can be made completely and refrigerated for up to 2 days in advance. Made-ahead or leftover soup can be reheated over gentle heat or served chilled.

Tamarind Margaritas

MAKES 2 DRINKS (REPEAT AS NEEDED!)

Tamarind makes a great addition to the classic margarita. Its tart flavor backs up the lime juice and plays off the sweetness of the Cointreau. This recipe makes 2 margaritas in a tall cocktail shaker filled with ice. If you're making them like that—two at a time—use the tablespoon and cup measurements. If you'd like to make a large batch of the mix before the party gets started and shake as you go, then multiply the ounce measurements as needed and use a liquid measuring cup to do the measuring. Store the batch of mix in the refrigerator and pour about 8 ounces (1 cup) into the shaker for each 2 drinks.

FOR THE SEASONED SALT (OPTIONAL):
¼ cup kosher or fine sea salt
¼ teaspoon chipotle powder, or to taste
½ lime, squeezed, and squeezed-out lime
   half reserved

—————

Ice cubes, as needed

¼ cup (2 ounces) silver tequila
2 tablespoons (1 ounce) Cointreau, triple
   sec, or other orange liqueur
2 tablespoons (1 ounce) tamarind puree
   (see Note)
Juice of ½ lime (see above)

1. If you're serving the margaritas with chile-salt–crusted rims, stir the salt and chipotle powder together on a small plate until blended. Rub the rims of 2 cocktail glasses with the squeezed-out lime half and press the rims of the glasses in the salt to lightly coat them.
2. Fill a cocktail shaker halfway with ice cubes and pour in the tequila, Cointreau, tamarind puree, and lime juice. Shake vigorously and strain into the glasses.

NOTE: Tamarind puree—not to be confused with tamarind syrup or tamarind pulp— is a smooth, unsweetened brownish-green puree. Look for it (bottled or frozen) in Asian and Latin markets and some well-stocked supermarkets. It is also available online at www .perfectpuree.com.

Preparation Schedule

2 days before the dinner:
- Make the watercress soup.
- Bone the ducks, cook the legs, and make the *sofrito* and the duck broth (steps 1 through 8 of *Arroz con Pato*).

1 day before the dinner:
- Marinate the seafood for the ceviche.

Up to 2 hours before guests arrive:
- Drain the ceviche and finish it with the grapefruit and herbs; keep refrigerated.
- Take cheeses out to bring to room temperature and prepare fruit.

Just before sitting at the table:
- Plate up the ceviche.
- Warm the soup.

After clearing the ceviche:
- Start the rice and cook it through to the point where the pot is covered.
- Start panfrying the duck breasts over low heat (you may have to excuse yourself to check them once or twice).
- Serve the soup.

After clearing the soup:
- Remove the rice from the heat when it is cooked.
- Finish cooking the duck breasts and let them rest.
- While the duck breasts are resting, crisp up the skin.
- Slice the duck breasts, assemble the plates, and serve.

CHAPTER SEVEN

'Tis the Season Festive Buffet

Serves 12

Tierrita Mía

Country-Style Spareribs with *Manchamanteles*

Shrimp *Diablo*

Arroz Mamposteado

Peruvian Salad

Coconut Tapioca with Mangoes

When my children were younger, I was able to juggle large parties at home because I mastered the art of preparing menus with "do-ahead" dishes in mind. I adore entertaining en masse during the holidays and have become quite adept at developing dishes that are conducive to the kind of entertaining I do. Not only are most of the recipes that make up this menu "do-ahead," they are better for having been made ahead of time and keep quite nicely. Even the components for the two dishes that require a little last-minute time—the rice and beans for the *Arroz Mamposteado* and the sauce for the Shrimp *Diablo*—can be done in advance.

When my family visited Peru, I came across a salad all along La Valle Sagrada that I couldn't get enough of. The Peruvian salad was made with baby lupini beans, which are known in Peru as *tarwi*. The texture of this salad is difficult to explain, because it is a bit toothy; but consider the crunchy piquancy of the radishes, the smokiness of the roasted peppers, and the herbal freshness of the cilantro and mint, all drizzled with some fruity olive oil and a squirt or two of lime, and you can understand why I wax poetic about this salad. Almost as good as the salad itself is the fact that the salad gets better if it sits at room temperature for a couple of hours.

As a die-hard Puerto Rican, I can't imagine the holidays without pork in some guise. The combination of the pork with a fruity mole in the Country-Style Spareribs with *Manchamanteles* fills the bill and, as if the succulence of this dish weren't enough, the fact that I make it days before I serve it (and it tastes even better!) is a deal closer for me.

This is hearty, wintertime comfort food that is made with virtually no last-minute stress. Even the old standby tapioca (made the day before, of course!) gets dressed up for the holidays with slices of fresh sunset-orange mangoes. Follow the preparation schedule on page 115 and you'll be setting your guests up for some very merry entertaining indeed.

Country-Style Spareribs with *Manchamanteles*

MAKES 12 BUFFET OR 8 MAIN-COURSE SERVINGS

The richness of country-style spareribs is perfectly matched to the slightly acidic, very fruity, and mildly spicy *manchamanteles* sauce. It is not only better to make these spareribs ahead, but I strongly recommend it. After a day or two in the refrigerator, it will be easier to remove the fat from the surface of the sauce, and the juices and flavor will have penetrated the ribs. When it comes to party time, all that's left to do is to reheat the ribs. The ribs will be fork-tender, the juices will have cooked down to a lovely, fruity glaze, and the whole thing can be served right from the baking dish.

7 to 8 pounds boneless country-style ribs, trimmed of most but not all excess fat

3 tablespoons Achiote Oil (page 135)

2 tablespoons cider vinegar

Adobo seasoning

2 tablespoons olive oil

6 cups *Manchamanteles* (page 29)

1. Cut the spareribs into single-serving-size pieces if necessary. Pat the ribs dry with paper towels and put them in a large bowl. Rub the achiote oil into all sides of the ribs with your hands, then sprinkle the vinegar over them and toss to mix. Season liberally with adobo, rubbing the seasoning into the pork and making sure all sides of the ribs are well seasoned. Let them stand at room temperature for 1 hour or cover and refrigerate for up to 2 days. (Hint: Two days is better!)
2. Preheat the oven to 400°F.
3. Heat the olive oil in a wide, heavy skillet over medium-high heat. Add as many of the seasoned ribs as will fit without touching. Brown them well on all sides, about 15 minutes total. Remove them to a 15 by 10-inch baking dish (or other dish in which they fit snugly in a single layer) and repeat with the remaining ribs.
4. Spoon the *manchamanteles* over the pork, wiggling the dish so the sauce works its way

Country-Style Spareribs with *Manchamanteles* and *Arroz Mamposteado.*

between the ribs. Cover the dish with a sheet of parchment paper and then a sheet of aluminum foil, crimping the foil to the sides of the dish to make a tight seal. Bake until the ribs are fork-tender, about 1¾ hours. Remove from the oven and let cool to room temperature. Refrigerate for 1 to 2 days. *(You could serve the ribs right away, but they will be noticeably better—the flavor will have permeated every inch of the ribs—after a couple of days. Also, the fat will rise to the top, making it easy to remove before reheating.)*

To serve:

5. Bring the ribs to room temperature. Meanwhile, preheat the oven to 350°F.

6. Spoon/scrape the fat from the top of the sauce and ribs. Bake the ribs, uncovered, for 20 minutes. Remove the baking dish from the oven and, very carefully, turn the ribs over in the sauce. Return to the oven until heated through, 20 to 25 minutes. (It's unlikely, but if the ribs appear even slightly dry, cover the dish after turning the ribs.) Spoon a little of the sauce over the ribs and serve them from the baking dish right away.

Shrimp *Diablo*

MAKES 12 BUFFET OR 6 MAIN-COURSE SERVINGS

There is something nice about having most of the work done for a dinner party—more time to party, less time in the kitchen. There is also something very nice about disappearing into the kitchen for a few minutes (and I mean minutes!) and emerging with a knockout dish. It adds a little restaurant-y drama to the evening, especially when the aromas of smoky chipotle chiles and sweet sautéed shrimp accompany you on your return. If the sauce is made ahead, you'll need about 5 minutes to cook and simmer the shrimp. Plan on a little longer for graciously accepting compliments.

FOR THE SAUCE:

2 tablespoons olive oil

1 cup *Sofrito* (page 134)

2 canned chipotles in adobo (and the adobo sauce from the can that clings to them), finely chopped

1¼ teaspoons ground cumin

4 cups canned chopped tomatoes, with juice

Kosher or fine sea salt

FOR THE SHRIMP:

3½ pounds jumbo shrimp (about 12 per pound), peeled and deveined

2½ teaspoons chipotle chile powder

3 tablespoons olive oil

Juice of 1 lime, or as needed

Make the sauce:

1. Heat the 2 tablespoons oil in a medium saucepan over medium heat. Add the *sofrito* and cook until the liquid has evaporated and the *sofrito* starts to sizzle. Stir in the chipotles and cumin and stir until it smells wonderful—just about 1 minute. Stir in the tomatoes, bring to a boil, and adjust the heat so the sauce is simmering. Season lightly with salt and cook until the sauce is thickened (just enough liquid to cover the tomatoes), about 20 minutes. The sauce may be made to this point up to 2 days in advance. Refrigerate in the saucepan and reheat to simmering over low heat.

Season and cook the shrimp:

2. Toss the shrimp and chipotle powder together in a bowl to coat the shrimp with the seasoning. The shrimp may be seasoned up to 2 hours before cooking. Refrigerate until needed.

3. Heat the 3 tablespoons oil in a large skillet over medium heat. Add the shrimp and toss until they begin to turn pink, 1 to 2 minutes. Pour in the sauce and bring to a boil. Adjust the heat so the sauce is simmering and cook just until the shrimp are opaque at the center, about 3 minutes. Stir in 1 tablespoon lime juice and season with salt and/or more lime juice to taste (if the sauce needs it). Serve right away.

Arroz Mamposteado (SEE PHOTO, PAGE 102)

("MUSHED-UP" RICE)

MAKES 12 BUFFET OR 6 GENEROUS SIDE-DISH SERVINGS

Many Latin countries, not surprisingly, have clever and delicious ways of using leftover plain white rice. Colombians make a breakfast of leftover rice and beans and call it *calentado* ("heated up"). *Arroz mamposteado,* which has always been a way of stretching the family food dollar in Puerto Rico, is the hot new thing on the island's restaurant scene. For less festive occasions, all you need to round this out into a full meal is a salad—as simple or as elaborate as you like.

FOR THE BEANS:

2 tablespoons vegetable oil

1½ cups diced (¼-inch) cooked ham

½ cup *Sofrito* (page 134)

½ teaspoon ground cumin

2 cups cooked pink beans (see Daisy Does, opposite); one 15.5-ounce can pink beans, drained and rinsed; or 2 cups any leftover cooked beans

1 cup homemade or store-bought chicken broth

⅓ cup homemade or store-bought tomato sauce

FOR THE RICE:

4 cups cooked white rice, preferably short-grain (see page 109)

2 tablespoons vegetable oil

1 medium onion, cut into ¼-inch dice (about 1½ cups)

½ medium red bell pepper, cut into ¼-inch dice (about ¾ cup)

Make the beans:

1. Heat the 2 tablespoons oil in a large skillet over medium-high heat. Add the ham and stir-fry until the ham is fragrant and starts to show color. Stir in the *sofrito* and cumin and cook, stirring, until the liquid has evaporated and the *sofrito* starts to sizzle. Add the beans, broth, and tomato sauce and bring to a boil. Adjust the heat so the liquid is simmering and cook until slightly thickened, about 5 minutes. The beans can be prepared up to 1 day in advance and refrigerated.

Make and season the rice:

2. The plain rice can be cooked up to 1 day in advance and refrigerated or cooked up to several hours ahead and left at room temperature.

3. Heat the 2 tablespoons oil over medium heat in a heavy pot large enough to hold both rice and beans. Add the onion and bell pepper and cook, stirring to prevent sticking, until the onion starts to soften, about 4 minutes. Add the rice and cook, stirring so the rice doesn't stick to the pan, until the rice is separated and warmed through. The rice and vegetables can be prepared up to 2 hours in advance and left at room temperature.

To finish the rice and beans:

4. Reheat the beans to simmering. Return the rice and vegetables to medium heat if necessary. Cook until warmed through. Stir the beans and their liquid into the rice, cover the pot, and reduce the heat to low. Cook until everything is heated through, 3 to 4 minutes. Serve immediately.

VARIATION: "Mushed-Up" Rice with Ripe Plantains

Stir 1 cup (or more, if you like) of sautéed sliced ripe plantains into the finished rice and beans. The sweetness of the plantains and the smoky meatiness of the ham make a delicious partnership.

DAISY DOES: **BEANS**

Whatever kind of dried bean you are preparing, from relatively quick-cooking types like black beans or navy beans to garbanzos, which can take a few hours to cook, the procedure is pretty much the same.

I know it's common kitchen wisdom that beans have to be soaked—overnight in cold water or a "quick soak" in hot water for an hour or so—but I never soak them. Well, almost never: Sometimes I will soak garbanzos (chickpeas) to shave half an hour or so off the cooking time and I soak lupini beans (see page 111) for the same reason as well as to remove some of their bitterness.

When I tell people that I don't soak beans, they usually respond that beans *have* to be soaked, or else they take forever to cook and will cook unevenly. It is true that soaked beans will cook a little faster than unsoaked beans, but we're talking minutes, not hours, and it doesn't seem worth it to me. As for cooking unevenly, follow these basic instructions and you'll end up with evenly cooked beans with a creamy texture and no "bones" (hard white centers):

Rinse the beans in a colander under cold running water. While you're at it, pick over the beans and remove the occasional pebble or funky-looking bean. Pour the beans into a heavy pot large enough to hold them and plenty of water. My favorite bean pot to cook 1 to 2 pounds of beans is a 6-quart enameled cast-iron Dutch oven. Pour in enough cold water to cover the beans by 2 inches. Don't add salt at this point. Add a couple of bay leaves and a ham hock or large smoked turkey wings if you aren't vegetarian and like a little smoke with your beans, like I do.

Bring the water to a boil, then adjust the heat so there is a happy bubble, not a full boil, and start skimming off the foam that rises to the top. Most beans will take about 2 hours to cook, give or take 15 minutes. During the first hour and a half, check the beans every once in a while to make sure they are covered by at least 1 inch of water. Add more water to keep them covered if necessary. When the beans are almost tender (somewhere around that 1½-hour mark), lower the heat to a simmer. Add at least 2 teaspoons of salt per pound of beans and continue cooking them until they are tender. Don't add any more liquid, but do keep an eye on the beans so they don't stick and scorch. The end result should be a pot of creamy-tender (not mushy!) beans and just enough liquid to generously coat them like a thick, silky sauce. Once they're done, you can leave the beans on the stove (but off the heat) for a couple of hours and reheat them gently when it's time to serve them.

Basic Rice

MAKES ABOUT 10 CUPS (6 TO 8 SERVINGS)

This very simple method, which I have been using since I can remember, will result in perfect rice whatever type of white rice you are preparing. Long-grain rice gives you separate, tender, fluffy grains; short- and medium-grain rice yield rice that is a little denser and with a little more chew. My rice of choice for the *Arroz Mamposteado* on page 106 is short-grain rice, which is also a nice change from the everyday.

> ¼ cup vegetable oil
>
> 4 cups long-grain, medium-grain, or short-grain rice
>
> 2 tablespoons kosher or fine sea salt

1. Heat the oil in a heavy 3- to 4-quart pot over medium heat. Add the rice and salt and stir until the rice looks "chalky" and is coated with oil. Pour enough water into the pot to cover the rice by 1 inch. Raise the heat to high, bring the water to a boil, and boil until the rice just starts to peek through the surface of the water.

2. Reduce the heat to very low, give the rice one very thorough stir, and cover the pot. Cook until the rice is tender but with a little bite, about 20 minutes. Do not uncover the pot or stir the rice while it cooks. Fluff with a fork before serving.

Peruvian Salad

(LUPINI BEANS, RADISHES, AND ROASTED PEPPERS)

MAKES 12 GENEROUS SERVINGS

Like pisco sours (page 69), a little portion of this salad appears automatically whenever you are seated at a restaurant table in Peru. The beans should have a little bite left to them, which plays nicely off the soft, sweet peppers and crisp, peppery radishes.

1 pound dried lupini beans (see Notes)

2 tablespoons kosher or fine sea salt, plus more for seasoning the salad

¼ cup olive oil

2½ tablespoons cider vinegar or red wine vinegar

Juice of 2 limes

Finely grated zest of 1 lime

4 medium yellow, orange, and/or red bell peppers (about 8 ounces each), roasted and diced (see Notes and Daisy Does, opposite)

1 large bunch radishes, trimmed and cut into more or less ⅓-inch dice (about 2 cups)

3 tablespoons chopped fresh cilantro

3 tablespoons chopped fresh mint

1. Soak the lupini beans overnight in enough cold water to cover generously.
2. The next morning, drain the beans and put them into a 4- to 5-quart pot. Pour in enough cold water to cover by 2 inches. Bring to a boil, then drain. Repeat 3 times.
3. Return the beans to the pot; add cold water to cover by 2 inches and the 2 tablespoons salt. Bring to a boil, then adjust the heat so the liquid is simmering. Cook until the beans are tender but still with a little bite, about 2 hours.
4. Drain the beans and put them in a serving bowl. Add the olive oil, vinegar, lime juice, and zest, and toss to coat. Add the roasted peppers (if using diced), radishes, cilantro, and mint and toss well; let stand at room temperature for up to 2 hours or refrigerate for up to 1 day before serving. If refrigerated, bring to room temperature before serving. In either case, taste the salad and add salt if necessary before serving.

NOTES

- In Peru, this would be made with tender, fresh young lupini beans, which are difficult to find in the States. Search out the smallest dried lupini you can and be advised: Even the smallest beans will still cook up with quite a bit of bite. That is the way they should be, more like a garbanzo in texture than a white bean.

- Adding diced roasted peppers to the salad makes it simple to eat in a buffet setting where some guests might be standing or balanced on the edge of an ottoman. If your guests are seated, you might want to spoon the finished salad into roasted pepper halves. (Roast 6 peppers [instead of the 4 called for above] as described below, but cut them in half lengthwise [through the stem] before seeding and cleaning them. Use the roasted pepper halves as cups to hold the salad.) If you are dicing the peppers and stirring them into the salad, feel free to substitute 2 cups diced (½-inch) bottled roasted peppers for the freshly roasted peppers. Be sure to drain bottled peppers thoroughly before dicing them.

DAISY DOES: ROASTED PEPPERS

Choose thick-fleshed, straight-sided yellow, red, or orange bell peppers. Light a burner of your gas stove (or the broiler; see below). Place the peppers directly over the flame and roast them until the skins are evenly blackened on all sides. Turn the peppers with a pair of long-handled tongs just as each side turns black, to prevent the peppers from overcooking.

If using the broiler, set the rack about 8 inches from the broiler and preheat the broiler (to high, if possible). Line up the peppers on the broiler rack and broil them, turning as necessary, until blackened on all sides. (Roasting the peppers can be done over hot coals, too.)

Carefully wrap each blackened pepper in a double thickness of well-dampened paper towel. Let the peppers stand until cool. *(The steam formed by wrapping the peppers in damp paper towels will loosen the skins and make them easier to remove.)* Cut the peppers in half lengthwise. Pull out the cores and stems, and scrape out the seeds and liquid. Turn the peppers over and scrape off the blackened skins. At this point, the peppers can be cut for use in recipes or stored in the refrigerator for up to 4 days, covered with a thin layer of olive oil.

Coconut Tapioca with Mangoes

MAKES 12 SERVINGS

A classic comfort-food dessert takes an exotic turn with the addition of coconut milk and slices of silky, ripe mango.

⅔ cup sugar

⅔ cup instant tapioca

Two 13.5-ounce cans unsweetened coconut milk

2½ cups light cream

2 large eggs, beaten

Finely grated zest of 2 limes, plus zest strips for serving, if you like

Large pinch of ground ginger

2 teaspoons vanilla extract

2 ripe(!) mangoes

1. Stir together all the ingredients except the vanilla and mangoes in a medium saucepan. Let stand for 5 minutes. Place over medium-low heat and cook, stirring constantly, until the tapioca comes to a full boil. Take off the heat and stir in the vanilla.

2. Divide the tapioca among twelve 6-ounce dessert dishes or pour it all into one serving bowl. Cover each dish or the bowl with plastic wrap, pressing the wrap directly onto the top of the tapioca to prevent a skin from forming. Let cool to room temperature, then refrigerate until completely chilled, at least 2 hours or up to 1 day.

3. Just before serving, stand each mango on its end and slice away the fruit on either side of the pit. Peel the mango "fillets" and cut them crosswise into very thin slices. Fan a few of the slices over the top of the tapioca in dessert dishes or decorate the top of the tapioca in a serving bowl with all of the slices.

Tierrita Mía

MAKES 4 DRINKS

This may sound like an odd name for a cocktail, but I borrowed the name and the flavors from *tierrita dulce,* a Puerto Rican dessert whose name translates into "sweet little earth." In my drink version, the rich flavors of chocolate, coffee, and rum are in perfect balance and the half-and-half helps mellow the whole thing out. To really send this over the top, whip up a little heavy cream, garnish each drink with a small dollop, and sprinkle some ground cinnamon over the whipped cream.

¾ cup Godiva or other chocolate liqueur
¼ cup plus 2 tablespoons half-and-half
3 tablespoons Kahlúa or other coffee
   liqueur

3 tablespoons dark rum
Crushed ice

1. Stir all the ingredients except the crushed ice together and chill for a day or two. The mix can be used right away, but the finished drinks are better if the mix is chilled first.
2. For each 2 drinks, fill a cocktail shaker about halfway with crushed ice. Pour in half the mix and shake vigorously. Strain into chilled cocktail glasses.

Preparation Schedule

3 to 4 days before the buffet:
- Make the *manchamanteles*.
- Marinate the spareribs.

2 days before the buffet:
- Sear and bake the spareribs.
- Make the sauce for the shrimp.
- Make the *Tierrita Mía* mix.

1 day before the buffet:
- Soak the lupini beans.
- Make the seasoned beans and cooked rice for the *mamposteado*.
- Make the tapioca.

4 to 6 hours before the buffet:
- Start cooking the beans; when they're done, assemble the salad.
- Cook the plain white rice. (Do not sauté it with the vegetables yet!)

2 hours before the buffet:
- Remove the ribs to room temperature and skim the fat from the surface of the sauce.
- Sauté the vegetables and rice.
- Cut mango slices for the dessert.
- Season the shrimp.

As guests arrive:
- Shake and serve the *Tierrita Mías*.
- Put the ribs in the oven to heat.

15 minutes before serving:
- Heat the ham mixture for the *mamposteado;* when it is simmering, add the rice and heat.
- Make the shrimp and put it in a serving bowl or on a platter.
- Check the seasoning of the salad before serving.
- Serve the ribs directly from the baking dish.

CHAPTER EIGHT

After-the-Gift-Giving Breakfast

Serves 6 (with leftovers)

A PAIR OF QUICHES:

Pisto Manchego Quiche

Potato, Fig, and Blue Cheese Quiche

Coquito Pancakes with Fruit Salsa (see page 124)

My *Abuela's* Hot Chocolate

Hibiscus Flower Tea

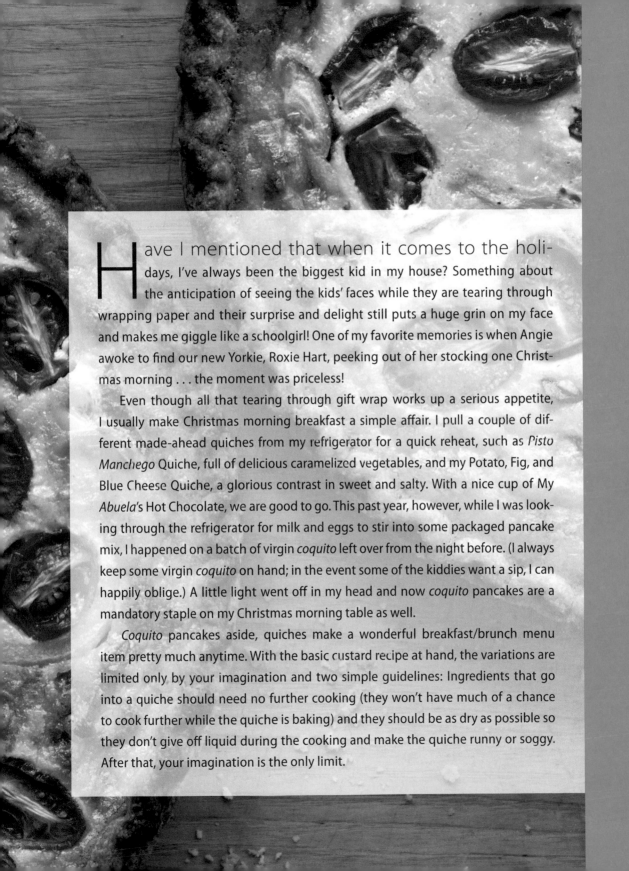

Have I mentioned that when it comes to the holidays, I've always been the biggest kid in my house? Something about the anticipation of seeing the kids' faces while they are tearing through wrapping paper and their surprise and delight still puts a huge grin on my face and makes me giggle like a schoolgirl! One of my favorite memories is when Angie awoke to find our new Yorkie, Roxie Hart, peeking out of her stocking one Christmas morning . . . the moment was priceless!

Even though all that tearing through gift wrap works up a serious appetite, I usually make Christmas morning breakfast a simple affair. I pull a couple of different made-ahead quiches from my refrigerator for a quick reheat, such as *Pisto Manchego* Quiche, full of delicious caramelized vegetables, and my Potato, Fig, and Blue Cheese Quiche, a glorious contrast in sweet and salty. With a nice cup of My *Abuela*'s Hot Chocolate, we are good to go. This past year, however, while I was looking through the refrigerator for milk and eggs to stir into some packaged pancake mix, I happened on a batch of virgin *coquito* left over from the night before. (I always keep some virgin *coquito* on hand; in the event some of the kiddies want a sip, I can happily oblige.) A little light went off in my head and now *coquito* pancakes are a mandatory staple on my Christmas morning table as well.

Coquito pancakes aside, quiches make a wonderful breakfast/brunch menu item pretty much anytime. With the basic custard recipe at hand, the variations are limited only by your imagination and two simple guidelines: Ingredients that go into a quiche should need no further cooking (they won't have much of a chance to cook further while the quiche is baking) and they should be as dry as possible so they don't give off liquid during the cooking and make the quiche runny or soggy. After that, your imagination is the only limit.

Pisto Manchego Quiche

MAKES TWO 9-INCH QUICHES (16 SLICES)

I think of *pisto manchego* as a Spanish version of ratatouille—a mix of eggplant, peppers, squash, onions, and tomatoes, with the occasional caramelized potatoes tossed in. It is a warm-weather favorite of mine. I love *pisto manchego* just about any way—on its own, as a base for poached eggs for brunch, or even tucked into a creamy-custardy quiche. *Pisto manchego* is all about the beauty of the raw ingredients that go into it. As for the herbs, feel free to play around: Add some parsley along with the thyme or a little pinch of very finely chopped fresh rosemary instead of the thyme.

Two 9-inch premade pie shells

1 large eggplant (about 1¼ pounds)

2 teaspoons kosher or fine sea salt, plus
more as needed

¼ cup olive oil

½ small onion, cut into ¼-inch slices
(about ½ cup)

1 medium-large zucchini (about 9 ounces),
topped and tailed and cut into quarters
lengthwise

1 teaspoon minced fresh thyme

Freshly ground pepper

2 cups heavy cream

4 extra-large eggs

Pinch of ground or freshly grated nutmeg

8 ounces smoked Gouda, coarsely
shredded (2 lightly packed cups)

¾ cup halved grape tomatoes

1. Prebake the pie shells (see Note).

2. Peel the eggplant and cut it into ½-inch cubes. Toss the cubes together with the 2 tea-spoons salt in a bowl. Let stand until some of the eggplant juices are drawn out, about 30 minutes.

3. Meanwhile, heat 1 tablespoon of the oil in a large skillet over medium heat. Add the onion and cook, stirring, until the onion is lightly browned and softened, about 8 minutes. Scoop the onion out of the pan into a bowl. Add the zucchini (and a little more oil if there isn't enough to coat the bottom of the pan), cut side down, to the pan and cook, turning as necessary, until all cut sides are browned, about 10 minutes. *(Browning the zucchini quarters before cutting them into cubes is easier than trying to brown all sides of the little cubes.)* Cut the zucchini crosswise into ½-inch pieces and add to the bowl with the onion. Remove the pan from the heat while you tend to the eggplant.

4. Blot the eggplant dry as thoroughly as possible. Turn the heat to medium-low. Add the remaining oil to the pan and swirl to coat the bottom. Add the eggplant and cook, stir-ring often, until the eggplant is browned on most sides, about 10 minutes. The eggplant should be tender to the bite but not mushy. Scrape into the bowl with the onion and zuke. Crumble the thyme into the bowl and season the vegetables to taste with salt and pepper, remembering that the eggplant has been salted already. Let cool to tepid. The shells and vegetable mix can be prepared up to several hours before baking the quiches and held at room temperature.

5. When ready to bake the quiches, preheat the oven or reduce the oven temperature to 350°F.

6. Make the custard: Beat the cream, eggs, ½ teaspoon salt, the nutmeg, and pepper to taste

together until smooth. Scatter a thin, even layer of cheese over the bottoms of both pre-baked shells. Divide the vegetable mix between the 2 shells, spreading it evenly over the cheese. Top with the remaining cheese. Put the quiches on a baking sheet large enough to hold them both comfortably and pour the custard into the shells. Decorate the tops with the tomato halves, cut side up. Bake until the edges of the custard are set and the center is only slightly jiggly, about 45 minutes.

7. Let the quiches cool for at least 15 minutes before serving. Serve warm or at room temperature. The quiches can be made the day before and refrigerated. Rewarm in a 300°F oven for 15 to 20 minutes before serving.

NOTE: To prebake the pie shells, preheat the oven to 425°F. Poke the bottoms of the shells all over with a fork. Line the shells with parchment paper or aluminum foil. Fill halfway with pie weights, uncooked rice, or dried beans. Bake the shells for 20 minutes. Remove from the oven and let cool. Reduce the oven temperature to 350°F if you are baking the quiches right away; if not, turn the oven off.

Potato, Fig, and Blue Cheese Quiche

MAKES TWO 9-INCH QUICHES (16 SLICES)

Two 9-inch premade pie shells

8 dried figs

1 small white onion (about 8 ounces)

3 to 4 tablespoons olive oil

1 Idaho potato (about 10 ounces), peeled and cut into ¼-inch slices

2 cups heavy cream

4 extra-large eggs

1 tablespoon finely chopped fresh chives

Pinch of freshly grated or ground nutmeg

Pinch of cayenne pepper

½ cup crumbled Cabrales or other blue cheese

1. Prebake the pie shells (see Note opposite).

2. Put the figs in a heatproof bowl. Pour in enough hot water to cover them completely and soak them until softened and plumped up, about 30 minutes.

3. When ready to bake the quiches, preheat the oven or reduce the oven temperature to 350°F.

4. Meanwhile, make decorative onion slices for the tops of the quiches: Cut the onion in half through the root and peel the halves. Cut one of the halves into very thin slices through the root end (the small piece of root left on the bottom will keep the slices attached). Stop when you have 12 nice even slices that hold together firmly at the root. Most likely you will use less than one of the halves; reserve the remaining onion for another use. Heat 1 tablespoon oil in a large skillet over medium heat. Add your nice onion slices and cook them, turning gently once, until well browned on both sides, about 5 minutes. Remove them to a plate.

5. Pour enough additional oil into the skillet to coat the bottom evenly. Add as many of the potato slices as will fit comfortably. Fry them, turning once, until browned on both sides and tender, about 7 minutes. Repeat with the remaining potato slices, removing them to the plate with the onion as they are done and adding a little more oil to the skillet if necessary.

6. Make the custard: Whisk the cream, eggs, chives, nutmeg, and cayenne together in a mixing bowl until well blended. Drain the figs and cut them into very thin slices.

7. Arrange half of the potato slices in an even layer over the bottoms of the prebaked shells. Scatter the figs and blue cheese evenly over the potatoes. Top with a second layer of potatoes. Put the quiches on a baking sheet large enough to hold them both comfortably and pour the custard into the shells. If any of the potatoes poke through the surface, submerge them. Decorate the tops with the browned onion slices. Bake until the edges of the custard are set and the center is only slightly jiggly, about 45 minutes.

8. Let the quiches cool for at least 15 minutes before serving. Serve warm or at room temperature. The quiches can be made the day before and refrigerated. Rewarm in a 300°F oven for 15 to 20 minutes before serving.

Hibiscus Flower Tea

MAKES 12 TO 16 SERVINGS

In zocalos (plazas) all over Mexico, local vendors set up little stands and sell fruits, vegetables, spices, and other essentials of daily life. I noticed on a trip to Oaxaca that there was always a line around the stand that sold *agua de jamaica,* a tea of steeped dried hibiscus flowers served cold. No wonder—in that blazing heat, hibiscus tea really quenched your thirst.

4 ounces (about 3 cups) dried hibiscus flowers (see Note)

1 cup agave nectar or honey, or to taste

Put the hibiscus flowers in a large heatproof bowl. Heat 10 cups water until hot (not boiling) and pour over the hibiscus. Let the tea steep until the water is cooled to room temperature, then strain the tea. Stir in the agave nectar and chill. Serve chilled, with or without ice.

NOTE: Dried hibiscus flowers are available in many Latin and Asian markets. You can also order them from Kalustyan's at www.kalustyans.com.

My *Abuela's* Hot Chocolate

MAKES 6 SERVINGS

During the summers I spent at my *Abuela* Clotilde's house in Puerto Rico, breakfast was pretty much the same every day: a soft-boiled egg, warm bread bought from a vendor who wheeled his cart by the house every morning, and a cup of hot chocolate. Mama Clotilde (as we called her) made her hot chocolate with milk, but I thought it would be nice made with coconut milk. The flavor of chocolate dominates, with the coconut adding a very subtle note. I love it just the way it is, but if you have a sweet tooth, add a little sugar to the finished hot chocolate.

One 25-ounce can or two 13.5-ounce cans
unsweetened coconut milk
½ cup heavy cream

8 to 9 ounces sweetened chocolate, such
as Cortes, Abuelita, or Ibarra (see Note),
broken into chunks

Empty the can(s) of coconut milk into a medium saucepan, scraping out the solids. Add the heavy cream and chocolate. Heat over low heat, stirring so the chocolate doesn't stick and scorch, just until steaming. Serve hot.

NOTE: Sweetened chocolate, sometimes flavored with cinnamon and/or vanilla, is common throughout Spanish-speaking countries. It can be used in baking and other dishes, but primarily it is meant for making hot chocolate. The chocolate that I grew up with, Cortes, is not flavored at all. Some brands, like Abuelita and Ibarra (both are flavored with cinnamon and vanilla), are sold as hexagonal tablets, 6 tablets to a box. Use about 3 tablets for the above recipe. Cortes and other brands are sold in long, half-kilo bars with ridges that make the bars easy to break into pieces. Try a couple of different brands to see which you prefer.

COQUITO PANCAKES WITH FRUIT SALSA

This happy accident came about when I found some virgin *coquito* (page 151) while rummaging around in the fridge to find some eggs and milk to add to the pancake mix. I figured, "Well, there's eggs and milk—three kinds of milk!—in *coquito,* so how bad can this turn out?" Turns out it was anything but bad and a new Christmas tradition was born. If you find yourself in the same boat, or want to whip up a really fantastic batch of pancakes, just start by measuring equal amounts of unspiked *coquito* and pancake mix into a bowl. Fiddle with the proportions if you need to in order to end up with a thick but pourable batter. Cook the pancakes the way you usually do, but keep an eye on the heat—the extra sugar in the batter may make them brown very quickly. Reduce the heat a notch if you see this happening.

Top the pancakes with a fruit salsa made with equal parts of diced kiwi, mango, and strawberry tossed with a spoonful or two of confectioners' sugar. Or if that seems too much like work, top them with butter, maple syrup, mango jam, and/or coarsely chopped pecans.

Preparation Schedule

1 day before the breakfast:
- Bake the quiche shells, make the fillings, and bake the quiches.
- Make the fruit topping for the pancakes.
- Steep the hibiscus tea.

20 minutes before the breakfast:
- Mix the pancakes.
- Reheat the quiches.
- Make the hot chocolate.

As guests sit:
- Make the pancakes.

CHAPTER NINE

Elegant
New Year's Eve Dinner

Serves 6

"Cherimoya" *Feliz*

~

Watercress, Red Pear, *Queso Fresco*, and Pomegranate Salad

~

Red Beet *Casonsei* with Poppy-Butter Sauce

~

Lobster with Sherried-Shallot Béchamel

Yellow Coconut-Serrano Rice

~

Guava Parfait with Raspberry Sauce

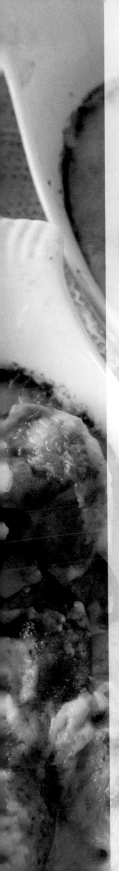

Growing up, New Year's Eve at my parents' house was always a festive event. *Mami* and *Papi* cooked for days leading up to the celebration. That evening, the house was inundated with family and friends, salsa records were spinning on the stereo, and *Papi* busted out his best merengue moves. It was something that the entire family looked forward to all year long. After I married and my parents retired to Florida, I didn't keep up the tradition, mainly because we lived in a small apartment and Jerry's schedule as a medical resident didn't permit it.

When my children were little and we moved from our apartment, New Year's Eve was once again spent at home. That night, I made a special "grown-up" dinner for the whole family before we tuned in to Dick Clark to watch the ball drop in Times Square. As they grew up, though, the boys started making their own plans for end-of-year celebrations. I still liked to celebrate the coming of a new year with a dinner that was a bit more festive than normal, so I'd have a few friends over to dine with Angela, Jerry, and me.

As I do other nights of the year, I like to change things up for New Year's Eve dinner from time to time, but this menu is definitely a keeper. The peppery Watercress, Red Pear, *Queso Fresco,* and Pomegranate Salad is a feast for the eyes right off the bat, but once you taste it, you know what true love is. You could easily go right to your entrée from there, but the easy-as-pie Red Beet *Casonsei* makes this a truly upscale event, showcasing the sweetness of the beets against the richness of the butter and the nutty crunch of the poppy seeds. Those *might* be Angela's favorite!

Reserved for a special night like this, Lobster with Sherried-Shallot Béchamel is creamy, fragrant, and luscious. The satiny sauce mellows the gentle heat of the Yellow Coconut-Serrano Rice, which is good enough to eat on its own. In fact, I like to serve this rice in warmer weather as well, when we fire up the grill at Casa Daisy; so you can enjoy it year-round with friends and family.

As always, most of the preparation for this menu can be done ahead. But there are last-minute touches—tossing the salad, saucing the *casonsei* with poppy seed butter, keeping an eye on the lobster as it bakes. But no worries; take your time as you move through this menu and savor every minute: This menu is meant to be enjoyed at a leisurely pace with your family and friends close at hand to ring out the old and ring in the new.

"Cherimoya" *Feliz*

MAKES 12 DRINKS

My indispensable assistant, Carolina, who has turned out to be quite the mixologist (just add that to her résumé!), waxes poetic whenever she describes one of her favorite fruit desserts from Chile, *cherimoya alegre* ("happy cherimoya"). It is very simply a diced cherimoya (also known as "custard apple" because of its creamy, sweet flesh) served with segments of orange and a dusting of confectioners' sugar—in a word, divine! Carolina came up with this delightful drink, but since cherimoya is very seasonal and difficult to find, I've substituted lychee nuts for the cherimoya for a close approximation in flavor. Soaking the lychees in brown sugar syrup, then floating them in sparkling wine, should make them pretty *feliz* indeed.

If you should happen to come across ripe cherimoya (most likely in the winter months), please try this drink with peeled and diced pieces of that fabulous fruit.

One 20-ounce can lychee nuts, drained
    and quartered
2 tablespoons light brown sugar

2 bottles moderately priced sparkling rosé,
    chilled

1. Toss the quartered lychees and brown sugar together in a small bowl, stirring every once in a while until the sugar has dissolved and the fruit starts to soak up the syrup, about 15 minutes.

2. Serve in champagne flutes: Divide half of the sweetened fruit mixture among 6 flutes, spooning it into the bottom of each flute. Put the rest of the fruit and syrup into a pretty glass pitcher. Pour 1 bottle of the rosé over the fruit in the glasses. Just before serving the second round, add the second bottle of rosé to the pitcher, tilting the pitcher as you pour in the wine.

Watercress, Red Pear, *Queso Fresco,* and Pomegranate Salad <small>(SEE PHOTO, PAGE 130)</small>

MAKES 6 GENEROUS OR 10 SMALLER SERVINGS

This is one festive-looking dish that's perfect for the winter holidays, but don't forget about it the rest of the year. Watercress is an amazing and versatile green. I don't think we use enough of it—in salads, sautéed as a vegetable side, or in soups (see page 97)—so I'm doing my bit to put it into more regular rotation. Sweet and juicy pear, crumbly-salty *queso fresco,* and tart pomegranate seeds help bring out the peppery quality of the cress.

3 bunches watercress

3 ripe but firm red pears

2 teaspoons fresh lemon juice

Seeds from 1 pomegranate, or 1 cup dried
  cherries (about 5 ounces)

1½ cups crumbled *queso fresco* (about
  6 ounces)

Kosher or fine sea salt and freshly ground
  pepper

⅔ cup extra-virgin olive oil

2 tablespoons sherry vinegar

1. Trim all the thick stems from the watercress. Wash the cress in cool water, then dry well, preferably in a salad spinner. The cress can be prepared up to 1 day in advance. Wrap it loosely in damp paper towels and store in a resealable plastic bag in the vegetable drawer of the refrigerator.

2. Quarter, core, and thinly slice the pears no more than 2 hours before serving and toss them with the lemon juice to keep them from turning brown. The seeds can be removed from the pomegranate up to a few hours before serving the salad.

3. Just before serving the salad, toss the watercress, pear slices, pomegranate seeds or cherries, and *queso fresco* together in a large serving bowl. Season lightly with salt and pepper, drizzle the oil over the salad, and toss well. Sprinkle the vinegar over the salad, toss well again, and serve right away.

Red Beet *Casonsei* with Poppy-Butter Sauce

MAKES ABOUT 4 CUPS FILLING (ENOUGH FOR ABOUT 90 *CASONSEI* [SEE NOTES])

Casonsei is a regional Italian word for ravioli. The beet and apple filling is fairly moist and will soak through the wrappers if the *casonsei* are made more than an hour or so in advance. The solution? Freeze them as soon as they are made and leave them in the freezer until you're ready to cook and serve them. *Gyoza* wrappers (or sturdy wonton wrappers) are a first-class shortcut for these and all ravioli.

FOR THE *CASONSEI*:

2 pounds medium beets (about 8), peeled and cut into 1-inch wedges

1 Granny Smith apple

Juice of 1 lemon

Kosher or fine sea salt and freshly ground pepper

About 100 (3½-inch) *gyoza* wrappers (about 1½ pounds; see Notes)

1 egg, well beaten

FOR SERVING:

8 tablespoons (1 stick) butter

1 tablespoon poppy seeds, plus more for sprinkling if needed

Grated Parmesan cheese

Make the filling:

1. Steam the beets over boiling water until tender, about 15 minutes. Drain the beets thoroughly and let them air dry for 15 minutes or so.

2. While the beets are cooling, peel the apple, cut it into quarters, and cut out the core. Cut the apple into roughly ½-inch pieces and toss together in a small bowl with the lemon juice. Put the apple and beets in a food processor and process until smooth. Scrape the filling into a bowl and season generously with salt and pepper. The filling can be made up to 1 day before making the *casonsei*.

Watercress, Red Pear, *Queso Fresco*, and Pomegranate Salad and
Red Beet *Casonsei* with Poppy-Butter Sauce.

Form the *casonsei*:

3. Before making the *casonsei,* line a baking sheet with a clean kitchen towel or parchment paper. Lay out 6 or 7 *gyoza* wrappers on your work surface. Using a pastry brush, moisten the edges of the wrappers with the beaten egg. Dab about 1½ teaspoons of the beet filling into the center of each wrapper. Bring the edges together to enclose the filling and make a half-moon shape. Pinch the edges sealed, paying special attention to the very ends of the half-moon shape. Lay the *casonsei* on the lined baking sheet as you form them. *(Make sure the* casonsei *aren't touching, or the dough will stick together and then tear when you try to separate them.)* When the tray is full, put it in the freezer. Repeat with the remaining wrappers and filling, using as many baking sheets as needed to give the *casonsei* enough space. When the *casonsei* are solid, transfer them to freezer-safe resealable plastic bags. The *casonsei* may be made and frozen up to 1 month in advance.

To serve:

4. Leave the *casonsei* in the freezer until you're ready to cook them. Heat a large pot of salted water to a boil. While the water is coming to a boil, melt the butter in a medium skillet over low heat and stir in the poppy seeds. Remove the skillet from the heat, cover, and keep warm in a warm corner of the stove.

5. When the water is at a rolling boil, slip 30 or 36 (plus a few to cover breakage) of the *casonsei* into the pot a few at a time. Stir them very gently and cook just until the centers of the *casonsei* are tender (the sealed edges should still be quite firm), 3 to 4 minutes. Very gently, scoop 5 or 6 *casonsei* out onto each warm serving plate, draining as much water off the *casonsei* as possible. *(Use a spider or wide skimmer for the best results.)* Spoon some of the poppy-butter over the *casonsei.* If a serving or two of the sauce looks a little shy of poppy seeds, sprinkle a few more onto the *casonsei.* Sprinkle Parmesan generously over the *casonsei* and serve right away.

NOTES

- About the yield: This recipe makes about 90 *casonsei,* or about three times as many *casonsei* as you will need for a second course for 6 guests in this menu. If cooking and serving the full amount, heat 2 pots of water to a boil and double the amount of poppy-butter sauce ingredients.
- I prefer *gyoza* wrappers to wonton wrappers for this recipe, as *gyoza* wrappers are slightly thicker and hold up better to the beet filling.

Yellow Coconut-Serrano Rice (SEE PHOTO, PAGE 137)

MAKES 6 GENEROUS SERVINGS

I have a friend from Honduras who puts a whole Scotch bonnet chile in with her *sofrito* when she makes rice. Her thinking is that as long as the chile stays whole, the heat it contributes to the rice will stay under control. (But if the chile should break and leak some of its seeds—the hottest part of any chile—into the rice, then you'd better look out!) I love the idea of a slightly spicy rice, but I'm taking a different approach here. I add a serrano chile to a pot of yellow rice made with coconut milk—a favorite way of making rice in the Caribbean. The coconut milk adds gentle sweetness to the rice and tempers the heat from the chile.

6 cups homemade or store-bought chicken broth, plus more as needed

One 13.5-ounce can unsweetened coconut milk

¼ cup Achiote Oil (page 135)

1 cup *Sofrito* (page 134)

¼ cup *alcaparrado* (see Note) or coarsely chopped pimiento-stuffed olives

1 serrano chile, stemmed and finely chopped (seeds and all)

2 tablespoons kosher or fine sea salt

4 cups long-grain rice

1. Heat the 6 cups broth and the coconut milk in a medium saucepan just until steaming. *(I don't usually heat the liquid before adding it to the rice, but if cooked too long, coconut milk can scorch and give the rice an off flavor. Heating the coconut milk–broth mixture beforehand means the liquid will come to a boil faster and cook down faster, lessening the chance of burning the coconut milk.)*

2. Heat the achiote oil in a 4- to 5-quart heavy pot or Dutch oven over medium heat. Add the *sofrito* and cook, stirring, until the liquid has evaporated and the *sofrito* is sizzling. Stir in the *alcaparrado,* chile, and salt and stir for a minute or two. Add the rice and stir until it is coated with the seasoned oil and the grains start to turn chalky. Increase the heat to medium-high and pour in the heated coconut milk and broth mixture. If there isn't enough liquid to cover the rice by the width of two fingers, add more broth as needed. Bring the liquid to a boil. Boil (without stirring!) until the liquid has boiled down to the level of the rice.

3. Reduce the heat to very low, cover the pot, and cook—*without lifting the lid*—until the liquid has been absorbed and the rice is tender, about 20 minutes. The rice can be held in a warm corner of the stove with the lid on for up to 45 minutes. Serve very hot or warm.

NOTE: *Alcaparrado* is a bottled condiment that contains coarsely chopped or whole green olives, chopped pimiento, and capers. It is available in Latin markets and most supermarkets with even a tiny Latin food section.

SOFRITO AND ACHIOTE OIL

At the risk of sounding like a drama queen, my life in the kitchen couldn't go on without *sofrito* and achiote oil. The first is an aromatic mix of onions, peppers, hot chiles, herbs, and tomatoes that adds a fresh zip to everything it touches. It's the way I start pots of yellow rice (see page 133), get *guisados* (stewy dishes with anything from chicken and beef to shrimp as the main ingredient) off and running, and lend a hand to old standbys like meatballs (see page 146) that are desperately stuck in a rut. In all of 15 minutes you can make and bag up enough *sofrito* to get you through at least half a dozen dishes and tuck those bags in the freezer.

Achiote oil is made with achiote (annatto) seeds: tiny, irregularly shaped, deep-brick-red seeds about the size of lentils. Steeping them in hot olive oil infuses the oil with a delicate aroma and gives it an orange-yellow color. Achiote oil lends a vibrant color and nutty flavor to rice, stews, and simple sautéed dishes. On its own or with a little help, like a few pressed cloves of garlic, it makes the simplest of rubs for grilling or roasting meats, poultry, fish, or vegetables.

Sofrito

MAKES ABOUT 4 CUPS

2 medium Spanish onions, cut into large chunks

3 to 4 cubanelle or Italian frying peppers, cored, seeded, and cut into chunks

16 to 20 cloves garlic, peeled

1 large bunch fresh cilantro

7 to 10 *ajíces dulces* (see Note)

4 *culantro* leaves (see Note)

3 to 4 ripe plum tomatoes, cored and cut into chunks

1 large red bell pepper, cored, seeded, and cut into chunks

Combine the onions and cubanelle or Italian peppers in the work bowl of a food processor and coarsely chop. With the motor running, add the remaining ingredients one at a time and process until smooth. The *sofrito* will keep in the refrigerator for up to 3 days. It also freezes beautifully: Spoon it into resealable plastic bags in 1-cup quantities.

> **NOTE:** *Ajíces dulces,* sometimes called *ajicitos,* are tiny peppers similar in appearance to habanero and Scotch bonnet peppers, but at the other end of the heat scale. They are sweet with a bright green, herbal flavor. *Culantro* is a leafy herb that smells and tastes like cilantro on steroids. Both *ajíces dulces* and *culantro* are available in Latin markets. If you cannot find one or both of them, simply leave them out and use 1½ bunches of cilantro.

Achiote Oil

MAKES ABOUT 1 CUP

Many countries in Latin America color and flavor their food with saffron. My preference for an equally beautiful color, subtler flavor, and a less expensive alternative is achiote oil (see box opposite).

> 1 cup olive oil
> 2 tablespoons achiote (annatto) seeds

Heat the oil and achiote seeds in a small skillet over medium heat just until the seeds give off a lively, steady sizzle. Don't overheat the mixture, or the seeds and the oil will both end up discolored and unusable. Once the seeds really get sizzling, remove the pan from the heat and let it stand until the sizzling stops. Strain the oil and discard the seeds. Store the oil for up to 4 days at room temperature in a jar with a tight-fitting lid.

Lobster with Sherried-Shallot Béchamel

MAKES 6 SERVINGS

When I was seventeen and landed my first big-girl job, I took my parents to El Faro in Greenwich Village (the oldest Spanish restaurant in New York City) to celebrate. *Mami* ordered a dish very similar to this on that visit—and on every other visit we made to El Faro. Aside from shelling the lobster, there is really nothing to this dish: just making a simple béchamel seasoned with shallots and sherry and keeping a careful eye on the casserole as it reheats and browns.

Six 1¾-pound lobsters

4 tablespoons (½ stick) butter, plus more
    for the baking dish

⅓ cup minced shallots

¼ cup all-purpose flour

4 cups milk

1 tablespoon dry sherry

Kosher salt and freshly ground pepper

Cook and shell the lobsters:

1. Bring a large pot of salted water to a boil. Carefully plunge 3 of the lobsters into the water headfirst and immediately cover the pot. Sneak a peek, and when the water returns to a boil, adjust the heat so the water is at a lively simmer. Cook until the lobsters are cooked through, 12 to 14 minutes after adding them to the pot. Remove the lobsters with long tongs to a colander in the sink. Repeat with the remaining lobsters. Let all the lobsters cool to room temperature.

2. Working over the sink, twist off the lobster tails and return them to the colander. Do the same to all the lobster claws. Discard the bodies or save them for making lobster broth. If you have a large, heavy knife (and are comfortable doing this), set the tails, hard-shell side up, on a cutting board. Cut them in half lengthwise right through the shell. Pick out the black vein that runs the length of the tail and pull the lobster meat from the half–tail

Lobster with Sherried-Shallot Béchamel and
Yellow Coconut-Serrano Rice.

shells. Or, using a pair of kitchen shears, cut along the underside edges of the shell to free the tail meat. Pull the meat from the shell in one piece, then cut in half lengthwise and remove the black vein. Using a nut or lobster cracker, crack the 2 knuckles and each claw and pull the meat gently from the shells, preferably in one piece. Let all the lobster meat drain on paper towel–lined baking sheets.

3. Butter a 15 by 10-inch baking dish (or use 6 small baking dishes). Arrange the tail meat, cut side down, over the bottom of the dish to cover it in a more or less even layer. Tuck the claw meat between the pieces of tail meat. Finally, scatter the knuckle meat evenly over the top. Cover the dish and refrigerate for up to a day.

Make the sauce and bake the lobster:

4. Preheat the oven to 425°F.

5. Heat the 4 tablespoons butter in a medium saucepan over medium-low heat until melted. Add the shallots and cook until softened, about 4 minutes. Stir in the flour and cook until the roux is bubbly, smooth, and thick—without taking on any color. Pour in 2 cups of the milk and whisk until smooth. Whisk in the sherry, then the remaining 2 cups milk, and continue whisking until the sauce is smooth and has thickened. Bring to a boil, lower the heat to a simmer, and cook for 4 to 5 minutes. Season generously with salt and pepper.

6. Spoon the hot sauce over the lobster and wiggle the dish so the sauce makes its way between the pieces of lobster. The lobster can be sauced and left at room temperature for up to 2 hours. Bake, uncovered, until the lobster is heated through, the edges of the sauce are bubbling, and the top is golden brown, about 15 minutes.

Guava Parfait with Raspberry Sauce

MAKES 6 SERVINGS

These parfaits are like individual, tropically inspired trifles. Like a lot of my favorite recipes, they are the end result of a lot of playing around in the kitchen. These started out as molded guava Bavarian creams (guava puree, lightened with whipped cream and firmed up with gelatin) on a base of sponge cake. I decided to lighten them up a little more and leave out the gelatin, but I found the guava–whipped cream mixture was a little too loose and that, as always happens with cream that is whipped ahead of time, it started to "water out" after a couple of hours. Then I remembered reading about "stabilized whipped cream" in Rose Levy Beranbaum's *Pie and Pastry Bible*. Some of the cream is heated with a little cornstarch to thicken it and then the thickened cream is slowly added to the rest of the cream as it is whipped. It is a neat little trick that works perfectly for this dessert. I use less cornstarch than Rose does because I was looking for a whipped cream that was soft enough to seep between the cake cubes, trifle style.

FOR THE RASPBERRY SAUCE (MAKES ABOUT 1 CUP):
One 10-ounce bag frozen raspberries
2 to 3 tablespoons sugar
2 teaspoons fresh lime juice, or to taste

FOR THE PARFAITS:
2 cups heavy cream
¼ cup confectioners' sugar
1 teaspoon cornstarch
2 teaspoons vanilla extract
1½ cups guava puree (see Note), chilled
Pineapple sponge cake (see page 15)
   or store-bought angel food cake or
   pound cake

Make the sauce:

1. Bring the raspberries, sugar, and ¼ cup water to a simmer in a small saucepan over medium-low heat, stirring until the sugar has dissolved. Pass the mixture through a fine sieve into a small bowl, scraping the fruit with the back of a spoon to pass as much sauce

through while keeping the seeds and pulp behind. Stir in the lime juice and chill. The sauce can be made up to 3 days in advance and refrigerated.

Make the guava cream and assemble the parfaits:

2. Heat ½ cup of the cream, the confectioners' sugar, and cornstarch in a small saucepan, whisking constantly, until the cream starts to bubble around the edges and is thickened. Remove from the heat and whisk in the vanilla. Set aside to cool.

3. When the thickened cream is cool, beat the remaining 1½ cups heavy cream in a medium bowl (a chilled bowl and beaters or whisk help) until frothy. Continue beating, gradually pouring in the cooled thickened cream, until the cream holds stiff peaks when the whisk is pulled from it. Gently fold in the guava puree until no streaks of white remain, cover the bowl, and refrigerate the guava cream.

4. Cut enough of the cake into ½-inch cubes to measure 6 cups. Pick six 10-ounce (or so) footed compote dishes or wide wineglasses and line them up on the table. Put ½ cup of the cake cubes in the bottom of each dish. Spoon 1 tablespoon of the raspberry sauce over the cake, making sure some of the sauce drizzles down the sides of the dish. Spoon a scant ⅓ cup of the guava cream into each dish and wiggle the dish to settle the cream. Repeat with another layer of cake, sauce, and guava cream. Cover the dishes individually and refrigerate them for up to 6 hours before serving. Serve chilled. If there is a little raspberry sauce left, drizzle some over the top of each parfait before serving.

NOTE: An excellent (but not cheap!) pink guava puree is available from The Perfect Purée of Napa Valley (www.perfectpuree.com). As an alternative, you may be able to find frozen Goya guava puree in your supermarket. Defrost the puree overnight in the refrigerator, then pass the puree through a very fine sieve using the back of a spoon. (Unsieved puree will be very grainy; the guava puree from Perfect Purée needs no sieving.)

Preparation Schedule

Up to 1 month before the dinner:
- Make the *casonsei* and freeze them.

The day before the dinner:
- Prepare the watercress for the salad.
- Make the raspberry sauce.
- Cook and shell the lobsters; arrange them in the baking dish and refrigerate.

Up to 6 hours before guests arrive:
- Make the guava parfaits.

2 hours before guests arrive:
- Prepare the pears, *queso fresco,* and pomegranate for the salad.
- Make the béchamel and top the lobster with it; leave at room temperature.

1 hour before guests arrive:
- Make the yellow rice; when it is done, cover it and keep warm on the stove.

As guests arrive:
- Make the "Cherimoya" *Feliz.*

Just before sitting down to dinner:
- Bring a pot of water to a boil for the *casonsei* and preheat the oven for the lobster.
- Assemble the salad and toss with the dressing.

After clearing the salad plates:
- Make the poppy-butter sauce, then put the *casonsei* in the pot to cook.

After clearing the pasta plates:
- Put the lobster in the oven to bake.

CHAPTER TEN

New Year's Day "Linner"

Serves 6

Coquito and "Choquito"

Sweet Plantain "Canoes" Filled with Shrimp *Diablo* (page 104)
or
Spaghetti and Chipotle-Pork Meatballs

"Casa de Steak" Salad

Rafael's Orange Panna Cotta

Everyone is familiar with brunch, but what about "linner," brunch's later-than-lunch-earlier-than-dinner counterpart? I think "linner" works wonderfully on New Year's Day, especially if you are recovering from a little bit too much New Year's Eve or if you don't do a big New Year's Eve and would like to make January 1 the big event.

I felt comfort foods that were satisfying and rich with flavor were the way to go with this menu, but I couldn't make up my mind between two favorites: Spaghetti with Chipotle-Pork Meatballs and Sweet Plantain "Canoes" Filled with Shrimp *Diablo*. Both are grown-up versions of little-girl favorites and both, when served with a salad that features crisp lettuce, radishes, and cukes, are a meal on their own. I'll let you decide.

Either way, and as usual with my menus, most of the preparation is done ahead. There are a few last-minute details like cooking the pasta and sautéing the shrimp, but nothing too involved to break the nice, relaxed feel of a leisurely New Year's Day meal. There will be plenty of time in the brand-new year to hurry up—take today to chill.

Sweet Plantain "Canoes" Filled with Shrimp *Diablo*

MAKES 6 SERVINGS

When I was a little girl, I went to the Essex Street market on Manhattan's Lower East Side every week with *Mami* and *Abuela*. The market was a terrific mix of kosher food stands, Latin prepared-food stands, and stalls that specialized in clothing and housewares. We carted home everything we needed to get us through a week of cooking. I helped schlep and my "fee" was a sweet ripe plantain, roasted whole in the skin until creamy, and filled with a spicy beef or pork *picadillo*. I've dressed the idea up a little bit, adding a shrimp filling in place of the *picadillo*, but the wonderful combination of salty and sweet that made these "canoes" a childhood favorite still remains. On less festive occasions, serve them with a salad for lunch or for dinner and call it a day.

Shrimp *Diablo* (page 104)
6 very ripe (black skin with just a flew flecks of yellow) plantains

1. Make the sauce for the Shrimp *Diablo* (up to 2 days in advance).
2. Starting at the stem end of the concave side of each plantain, make a daisy-petal-shaped cut from the stem to the opposite end; the cut should be wider at the center and taper toward the two ends of the plantain. Cut just through the skin, but not into the plantain. Leave the cutout "petal" of skin in place until the plantains are cooked and ready for stuffing.
3. Soak 6 separate sheets of paper towels in warm water and squeeze out most of the excess water. (The paper towels should be wet, but not dripping wet.) Wrap each plantain in a sheet of paper towel and cook them all on high in the microwave oven until the flesh is creamy-looking, not dry and starchy (lift an end of the "petal" to check), 7 to 9 minutes, depending on how ripe the plantains are. It is likely some plantains will take longer than others. If some of the plantains aren't ready after 7 minutes of cooking, dampen the paper towels again, rewrap the undercooked plantains, and continue cooking in 1-minute increments until they're done.
4. Work with one plantain at a time and keep the rest covered with aluminum foil to keep them warm. Peel off the "petal" from each plantain and discard it, but leave the rest of the skin in place. With a paring knife, start at one end of the opening and cut the plantain

in half lengthwise without cutting through the bottom skin. Gently separate the 2 halves of the plantain to make a pocket for the shrimp filling. Stand the plantains up on a baking sheet "petal" side up, and give them a firm little push so they stand on their own. Tent with aluminum foil to keep warm.

5. Make the shrimp and remove the pan from the heat. Put each plantain onto a serving plate and spoon some of the shrimp and sauce into each. Serve immediately.

Spaghetti and Chipotle-Pork Meatballs

**MAKES ABOUT 16 MEATBALLS AND 6 CUPS SAUCE
(6 SERVINGS PLUS LEFTOVER SAUCE AND MEATBALLS)**

I usually make meat sauce or meatballs for spaghetti the way my mother does—with an addition of *sofrito* (page 134), which gives another level of flavor to the finished dish. (The *sofrito* helps keep the meatballs moist, too.) When I discovered chipotle chiles, with their blast of heat and smoky flavor, I immediately thought of adding a little bit of those to the meatball mix instead. Made small (see Variation), they are perfect cocktail party food—easy to eat and substantial enough to count as "real" food.

FOR THE MEATBALLS:

1 medium yellow onion, coarsely chopped

2 canned chipotle chiles in adobo, minced, plus 2 tablespoons of the adobo sauce

3 cloves garlic, minced

1½ tablespoons very finely chopped fresh mint

1½ tablespoons very finely chopped fresh cilantro

1½ pounds ground pork

½ cup dried bread crumbs

1 large egg, beaten

2 tablespoons finely shredded *cotija* or Parmesan cheese

2 to 3 teaspoons kosher or fine sea salt

½ teaspoon freshly ground pepper

FOR THE SAUCE:

3 tablespoons olive oil

3 cloves garlic, minced

Two 28-ounce cans crushed tomatoes

1 bay leaf

½ teaspoon red pepper flakes

1 pound spaghetti

Grated Parmesan cheese, for serving

---

1. Preheat the oven to 375°F.

Make the meatballs:

2. Put the onion in a food processor and process to a puree. Scrape the onion into a large mixing bowl and stir in the chipotles and their adobo, the garlic, mint, and cilantro. Crumble the ground pork into the bowl and mix well with the onion mixture using your hands. Add the bread crumbs, egg, cheese, salt, pepper, and 3 tablespoons water and mix well. Shape the mix into 2-inch meatballs, lining them up on a rimmed baking sheet as you go. Bake until the meatballs are cooked through and lightly browned, about 30 minutes.

Make the sauce:

3. When the meatballs are done baking, heat the olive oil in a 4-quart saucepan or Dutch oven over medium heat. Add the garlic and stir for a few minutes, just until fragrant. Add the crushed tomatoes, bay leaf, and red pepper flakes. Drain the fat from the meatballs and add the meatballs to the pot. Bring the sauce to a boil over medium-high heat. Adjust the heat so the sauce is simmering and cook until the sauce is slightly thickened, about 30 minutes. The meatballs and sauce can be prepared up to 3 days in advance and refrigerated.

4. Just before serving, bring a large pot of salted water to a boil. Heat the sauce and meatballs to a simmer if they've been refrigerated. Stir the spaghetti into the boiling water and cook, stirring—especially for the first minute or two—until the pasta is cooked to your liking. Drain the pasta and transfer it to a large serving platter. Spoon some of the sauce over the spaghetti and top with some of the meatballs. Sprinkle a generous amount of Parmesan over the spaghetti and meatballs. Pass the remaining sauce, meatballs, and Parmesan separately.

VARIATION: Cocktail Meatballs (see photo, page 56)

Make the meatball mixture as above and shape it into 1½-inch meatballs, using 2 tablespoons of the mix for each. Bake them until browned and cooked through, 15 to 20 minutes, and then cook in the sauce as directed above. Serve the meatballs hot, with some of the sauce for dipping and decorative wooden picks or skewers for spearing the meatballs. Makes about 40 mini meatballs.

"Casa de Steak" Salad

MAKES 6 SERVINGS

Picture a typical steak house salad. Now imagine that salad on vacation in Latin America and you've got a good idea of this mix. Blue cheese and bacon give it steak house cred; tart Mexican *crema* gives it a little edge; and the mesclun lightens up the whole salad without making it wimpy. As for radishes, let's just say I can eat them like Rapunzel's mother.

FOR THE DRESSING:

1 cup *crema* (see Note) or sour cream

½ cup mayonnaise

Juice and finely grated zest of 1 lime

1½ cups crumbled Cabrales or other blue cheese (about 5 ounces)

Freshly ground pepper

FOR THE SALAD:

1 pound slab bacon

One 5-ounce container "spring mix" greens or mesclun

1 bunch radishes, trimmed and cut into very thin slices (about 2 cups)

1 large English (hothouse) cucumber, cut in half lengthwise, seeded, then cut into ½-inch dice (2 generous cups)

2 tablespoons olive oil

Kosher or fine sea salt and freshly ground pepper

Make the dressing:

1. Whisk the *crema*, mayonnaise, and lime juice and zest together in a small bowl until smooth. Fold in the Cabrales and season with pepper to taste. The dressing may be made up to 2 days in advance. Cover and refrigerate. Bring to room temperature before serving.

Prepare the salad ingredients:

2. If necessary, cut the rind off the bacon. Cut the bacon into ¼-inch slices and then cut the slices crosswise into ¼-inch lardoons. Put the lardoons into a large skillet with 2 tablespoons water. Set over high heat and cook until the water has evaporated and the bacon

starts to sizzle. Reduce the heat to low and cook until the bacon is lightly browned but not at all dried out, about 6 minutes. Transfer the bacon to a paper towel–lined plate to drain. Discard the fat or save for another use. The bacon can be cooked several hours before serving the salad and kept at room temperature (don't refrigerate).

3. Wash the salad greens and dry them well, preferably in a salad spinner. The greens can be wrapped in damp paper towels and stored in a resealable plastic bag in the refrigerator for up to 1 day. The radishes and cucumber can be prepared up to several hours before serving and refrigerated. *(The radishes will stay nice and crisp in a bowl of ice water. Drain the radishes thoroughly before putting the salad together.)*

Toss and serve the salad:

4. Toss the greens, bacon, cucumber, and radishes together with the 2 tablespoons olive oil in a serving bowl. Season the salad lightly with salt and pepper and toss again. Serve the salad with the dressing on the side, letting guests help themselves to both.

NOTE: *Crema mexicana* is a tart dairy product with a consistency thin enough for spooning or drizzling. A drizzle adds a creamy-sour note to finished dishes like soups and stews, and a cupful serves as the base for dressings like this one. *Crema* is available in Latin groceries and larger supermarkets (check the dairy aisle, near the Latino cheeses). If you can't find *crema*, substitute sour cream thinned down with enough water so it drips easily from the spoon.

Rafael's Orange Panna Cotta

MAKES 6 SERVINGS

As much as I love to cook, every once in a while I like to get out from behind the stove and sit at the table instead. Recently, my good friend Jimmy Johnson invited me to his home, where he and his friends prepared a beautiful dinner for Jerry and me. The head chef, Rafael Fernandez, is a charming man from Argentina and no stranger to the kitchen, as he had run his own kitchen in many restaurants. As our chef for the evening, he explained that this was his grandmother's recipe, imported from Italy, and that he took great pride in it every time he made it. Now I celebrate his *nonna* every time I make it as well!

Heads up: This is a very soft-textured panna cotta. There is just enough gelatin in the cream mixture to set it. Once unmolded, it won't have perfectly straight sides or a smooth, even top, but it will have the most delicious texture and flavor!

Unsalted butter, for the ramekins

½ cup plus 1 tablespoon granulated sugar

2 cups heavy cream

½ cup plus 1 teaspoon confectioners' sugar

½ vanilla bean, cut in half lengthwise

Grated zest of 1 orange

¼ cup cold milk

1 package unflavored gelatin

3 tablespoons orange or tangerine liqueur

1½ teaspoons orange flower water (see Note)

1 teaspoon fresh lemon juice

1. Lightly butter six 6-ounce ramekins or custard cups and set them aside on a heatproof surface.

2. Make the caramel: Mound the ½ cup granulated sugar in the center of a medium, heavy skillet. Pour ¼ cup water around the sugar and place the skillet over medium heat. Swirl the pan to completely dissolve the sugar as the liquid heats. Continue swirling the pan— but don't stir the syrup!—until the sugar starts to change color. Continue swirling so the caramel colors evenly, until the caramel is a light copper color. Immediately pour the caramel into the bottom of the prepared ramekins, dividing it evenly. Don't handle the ramekins until the caramel has had a chance to cool.

3. While the caramel is cooling, stir 1 cup of the heavy cream, the ½ cup confectioners' sugar, the vanilla bean, and the orange zest together in a small saucepan. Bring just to a boil over medium heat. Remove the saucepan from the heat and let cool to tepid. Repeat the boiling/cooling process 2 more times and then strain the cream into a medium bowl. Discard the vanilla bean and orange zest.

4. Put the milk in a small bowl and sprinkle the gelatin over the surface. Let stand until the gelatin has softened. Whisk the orange liqueur, orange flower water, and lemon juice into the milk mixture, then stir the milk mixture into the strained cream and stir until the gelatin is completely dissolved, with no grains remaining. Transfer all this to a large mixing bowl and let cool to room temperature.

5. Pour the remaining 1 cup cream into a chilled bowl. Add the 1 tablespoon granulated sugar and 1 teaspoon confectioners' sugar. With a whisk or an electric mixer, beat the cream until it holds stiff peaks. Fold one third of the whipped cream gently into the cooled cream mixture with a rubber spatula. Fold in the rest of the whipped cream just until no white streaks remain and ladle the cream mixture into the prepared ramekins. Tap the ramekins on the counter to even them out and refrigerate for at least 4 hours or up to 1 day.

6. To serve, run a thin-bladed knife around the sides of each ramekin. Invert each ramekin over a dessert plate. Wait a few seconds and the panna cotta will slip right out and onto the plate. With a rubber spatula, scrape out any liquid caramel from the ramekin over the top of the panna cotta.

NOTE: Orange flower water is a clear, aromatic liquid distilled from fresh orange blossoms. The best-quality orange flower water can be pricey, but it's worth it. Look for orange flower water in Middle Eastern, Greek, and Arab groceries and well-stocked supermarkets and specialty food stores.

Coquito and *"Choquito"*

MAKES ABOUT 8 CUPS

Coquito is a ridiculously rich Puerto Rican version of eggnog made with coconut cream, eggs, sweetened condensed milk, and heavy cream. Oh, I almost forgot the rum and evaporated milk! Clearly not an everyday drink, this is a must in our household around the holidays.

As for *"choquito,"* the chocolaty cousin of *coquito* (see Variation), I have only one question: Why didn't anyone think of this before? Add chocolate to the mix and you've got yourself an absolutely knockout adult beverage with a rich, sensual texture and a gorgeous color. Of course, either version can be made without rum for kids and anyone else who would rather do without.

2 jumbo eggs (see Note)

3 jumbo egg yolks

One 14-ounce can sweetened condensed milk

One 15-ounce can cream of coconut (Coco López or other)

One 12-ounce can evaporated milk

1 cup heavy cream

¾ to 1 cup light rum

Ground cinnamon, for serving

1. Put the eggs and yolks in a blender jar. Blend at high speed until the eggs are pale yellow and very light. With the motor running, add the condensed milk, cream of coconut, and evaporated milk, one at a time and each in a very thin stream. Blend for a minute or so, then add the heavy cream in a slow, steady stream. Blend just until incorporated. If your blender jar becomes too full, simply pour some of the *coquito*-in-progress out into a serving pitcher and continue adding the milk/cream to what's left in the blender. When finished, pour what's in the blender jar into the serving pitcher and stir all together. Stir in the rum.

2. Chill for at least 2 hours or up to 6 hours. Serve in little coffee or tea cups and sprinkle a little cinnamon over the *coquito* before serving.

NOTE: If you are concerned about eating raw eggs, you can use pasteurized egg substitute with wonderful results. Also, buying super-fresh eggs from a reliable source and washing the shells well before using the eggs may reduce any risk of infection. In any case, pregnant women and those with a compromised immune system should avoid raw eggs.

VARIATION: *"Choquito"*

Prepare the *coquito* as described above. Before chilling it, heat ½ cup heavy cream in a medium saucepan until little bubbles form around the edges and the cream is steaming. Add 1½ cups bittersweet chocolate chips, let stand for a minute or two, then whisk until the chocolate is melted and smooth. Whisk about 2 cups of the *coquito* into the chocolate cream, then whisk that mix into the *coquito*. Chill and serve as above.

Preparation Schedule

Up to 3 days before the "linner" (or up to 3 weeks, if freezing):
- Make the meatballs and sauce, if serving.

The day before the "linner":
- Make the panna cotta.
- Make the salad dressing and prepare all the salad ingredients except the bacon.
- Make the sauce for the shrimp, if serving.

Early on the day of the "linner":
- Make the *coquito* or *"choquito."*
- Cook the bacon for the salad.

Just before guests arrive:
- Put a large pot of water on to boil and rewarm the meatballs and sauce, if serving.
- Season the shrimp, if serving.

Just before sitting down to "linner":
- Toss the salad ingredients (leave the dressing on the side).
- Cook the spaghetti, if serving.
- Microwave the plantains and, while they're cooking, sauté the shrimp, if serving.

ROSCA DE REYES

~

I couldn't write a book about the holidays without including the traditional *rosca de reyes*. When I was a little girl, *Mami* would tell me stories about *her* Christmases as a child and how Santa Claus didn't visit Puerto Rico because there was no snow for his sled to land on. (Imagine my horror at the thought of no Santa!) Instead, children who were good all year would be rewarded with a visit from the three kings on *Día de Reyes* (Feast of the Epiphany), January 6. *"Día de Reyes?"* I asked, my eyes wide with wonder. *Mami* explained that on the night of January 5, children put shoe boxes full of grass under their beds as a treat for the camels the three kings rode. The camels ate the grass and the kings would leave gifts and sweets for the children. "Why don't the kings visit us in Brooklyn?" I asked. "Well, for the opposite reason Santa doesn't go to Puerto Rico . . . the camels don't do snow!"

Rosca de Reyes is a delicious, slightly sweet yeast bread filled with orange-scented ground almonds and garnished with nuts and candied fruit. It is a tradition that made its way to the New World by way of Spain, where it is enjoyed with a steaming cup of hot chocolate. *Rosca* celebrates the three wise men who traveled to pay tribute to the infant Jesus at the time of his birth in Bethlehem. Traditionally, a small ceramic or plastic figure of the infant is hidden somewhere in the filling of the bread; whoever finds the infant is responsible for new swaddling for the figure of the infant on *El Día de la Candelaria,* or Candlemas, February 2. (Today, a dried bean often replaces the ceramic figure.)

In Mexico, the tradition has been modified a bit: The person who finds the hidden figure in the bread is responsible for making the tamales for the Candlemas celebration. Whether in Spain, Mexico, or any other country in Latin America that keeps this lovely tradition, *rosca* is a truly delicious addition to any breakfast or brunch as well as a satisfying simple snack and is certainly delightful enough to be enjoyed all year round.

Rosca de Reyes (SEE PHOTO, PAGE 157)

TRADITIONAL SWEET BREAD FOR EPIPHANY—*DÍA DE REYES*

MAKES 16 SERVINGS

FOR THE DOUGH:

1 package active dry yeast

½ cup milk

½ cup sugar

8 tablespoons (1 stick) unsalted butter, cut into 4 pieces

1 teaspoon kosher or fine sea salt

1 tablespoon vanilla extract

3 large eggs

3½ cups all-purpose flour, plus more for dusting

Finely grated zest of 2 oranges

Finely grated zest of 1 lemon

FOR THE FILLING:

2 cups almond flour (see Note)

½ cup sugar

2 tablespoons orange flower water (see Note, page 151)

2 tablespoons fresh orange juice

1 teaspoon ground cinnamon

½ teaspoon almond extract

———————————

1 dried bean

FOR DECORATING THE *ROSCA*:

1 large egg

1 tablespoon milk

Sliced almonds

Candied fruit and/or citrus peel, cut into little dice, strips, or any shape you like

Sugar

Make the dough:

1. Stir the yeast and 2 tablespoons warm water together in a small bowl. Let stand until foamy, about 10 minutes.

2. Meanwhile, heat the milk, sugar, butter, and salt together in a small saucepan over low heat just until the milk starts to steam—do not let it scald. Set aside until the temperature returns to about 110°F (slightly warmer than body temperature).

3. Stir the vanilla and yeast mixture into the milk mixture. Beat the eggs lightly in a small mixing bowl, then add the milk mixture to the beaten eggs, whisking constantly. Put the 3½ cups flour and the orange and lemon zests into the bowl of a standing mixer fitted with the paddle attachment. Turn the mixer to low and slowly pour in the egg milk mixture. Mix

just until the dough is blended. Do not overbeat; you want a well-incorporated, smooth, but still soft dough. Using a rubber spatula, scrape the dough out onto a well-floured surface.

4. Knead the dough gently, adding just enough flour to keep the dough from sticking to the work surface and your hands, until it is smooth and stretchy, about 5 minutes. Shape the dough into a ball, place it in a well-oiled bowl, then flip the ball over so all surfaces are oiled. Cover the bowl with a clean kitchen towel and set aside in a warm spot in the kitchen until the dough is doubled in size, 1 to 1½ hours.

Make the filling:

5. Stir the almond flour, sugar, orange flower water, orange juice, cinnamon, and almond extract together with a fork until the almond flour and sugar are evenly moist.

Shape, decorate, and bake the *rosca*:

6. Punch down the dough and roll it out on a well-floured surface to a rectangle about 20 by18 inches with one of the long sides closest to you. Crumble the almond filling over the dough, leaving an uncovered border of about 2 inches along the far side of the rectangle and 1 inch along both shorter edges. Place the bean somewhere over the filling.

7. Starting with the long end closest to you, start to gently roll up the dough and filling. Work back and forth along the length of the dough to roll it up evenly. Pinch the seam firmly along the length of the roll to seal it. Pinch closed both short ends. Join the two ends of the roll together to form a ring. Pinch the ends together to seal them tightly. Gently transfer the ring of dough to an oiled baking sheet.

8. Cover with the towel and set aside to rise until doubled in bulk again, 30 to 45 minutes.

9. Meanwhile, preheat the oven to 350°F.

10. To decorate, beat the egg and milk together until blended. Brush all sides of the dough with the egg wash. Decorate with sliced almonds, candied fruit, and/or citrus peel (they will stick to the egg wash). Brush the dough and decorations carefully again with the egg wash, then sprinkle liberally with sugar. Bake until the *rosca* is a deep golden brown, and the bottom sounds somewhat hollow when you thump it with your finger, 35 to 40 minutes.

11. Let cool for at least 45 minutes before slicing. (Be sure to warn your guests about the bean!)

NOTE: Almond flour is finely ground blanched (i.e., peeled) raw almonds. It is available in health food stores and well-stocked groceries, and via the Internet from Bob's Red Mill (www .bobsredmill.com). Or make your own: Grind whole blanched almonds in a food processor. Chill the almonds first and grind in small batches to keep the flour from becoming oily and gummy.

ACKNOWLEDGMENTS

I still can't believe that I was able to put this book together so quickly, but I do know that I never would have been able to do it without my right-hand man, Chris Styler. Chris, thank you again for your good humor, love, support, and guidance. I cherish our friendship always.

My team at Atria gets a huge round of applause. Judith Curr: fashionista, brilliant publisher, and role model, thank you for your vision and support. Johanna "Belleza" Castillo, who is never too busy to answer a call or lend a shoulder, even on her days off! Amy Tannenbaum gets a shout-out for her incredible attention to detail; Sybil Pincus, production editor; Dana Sloan and Kyoko Watanabe for the beautiful design and artwork in the book.

Carolina Peñafiel gets a great big thank-you for her tireless commitment, recipe testing, schlepping, managing, driving, cooking, mixing drinks, reminding me to laugh, and introducing me to La Vicky, her fabulous mother.

Thanks to my team of honorary "recipe testers": Lee and Loni Shomstein, Violette Tonuzi, Esmeralda and Frank Cantor, Jimmy Johnson (for his delicious contribution of NGB organic honey), and Rafael Fernandez and Yrving Torrealba for sharing their family recipes with me.

As always, last but not least, I thank my beautiful family—Jerry, Erik, Marc, David, and Angela, and, of course, Mami and Papi (who taught me how to do it right)—without whose love and inspiration I could not have written this book, and who allow me to create memories for them, each and every holiday.

INDEX

(Page references in *italics* refer to photographs.)

MORE FROM
DAISY MARTINEZ...

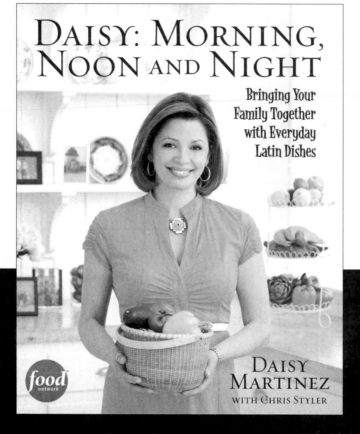

DAISY: MORNING, NOON AND NIGHT

Bringing Your Family Together with Everyday Latin Dishes

DAISY MARTINEZ
WITH CHRIS STYLER

"Daisy's authentic recipes are easy to make, easy to eat, and sure to please." —Rachael Ray

"Passion, tradition, flavor, and, most important, love—those are Daisy's main ingredients."
—Ted Allen, host of *Chopped* on the Food Network